COUNTING CHICKENS

Tales of Raising 8 Kids (and 4 Hens) in the City of St. Louis

by Jeff Fister

ISBN: 978-1-891442-50-6 • $13.95

Library of Congress Control Number: Pending

Editor: Jeannette Cooperman
Cover & book layout designed by Ben Pierce
Author photo by Jim Tobin

Printed in the United States of America

Virginia Publishing Company
PO Box 4538
St. Louis, MO 63108
www.STL-Books.com

For Laura

12.12.09

ACKNOWLEDGEMENTS

Many people along the way have encouraged me to put together a book of my *West End Word* columns. Well, at least some people. I ignored them long enough, so here it is. My deepest gratitude goes to my wife Laura, who really is the secret of the success of our family. Thanks also to my kids, who let me write about them; to my own parents for their support over the years; to my employees at Virginia Publishing, including book designer Ben Pierce; to Jeannette Cooperman, for editing help and consulting; to Kimberly Marlowe and Heather Navarro, two people who encouraged me to write this; and to my friends, neighbors and business associates.

TABLE OF CONTENTS

FOREWORD

Let's face it; writing a newspaper column isn't always easy. I've been writing one for my newspaper, the *West End Word*, for more than 20 years, and sometimes the "well" of creative ideas can run dry. I wrote about my neighborhood, my attempts to fix my old house and occasionally one in which I had to actually call someone and interview them (like in real journalism).

So how do I get an endless source of material?

I have eight kids.

Yes, writing about your kids is great because, well, they're right there and research time is minimal. And readers can relate because many people have kids and most people were a kid at one time.

And when I needed more material?

I raised chickens.

When we first started having chickens in our city backyard six years ago, we were quite unusual. Now there's a whole new "urban chicken movement" and more and more people know someone with chickens on their block.

But as I approach my 50th birthday with a 24 year-old son out in the working world (yes, it happens) and a four-year old preschooler at home, it's still the kids I come back to.

When I grew up, large Catholic families of six, eight or even 12 kids weren't unusual. Having eight now seems like a lot; I usually win that conversation at cocktail parties when someone asks, "How many kids do you have?"

And having that many has created some interesting symmetry. We call our oldest four kids the "bigs" and the second set the "littles." I realized at an event recently with the four "littles" that I had been to the same event 10 years ago with the four "bigs." And the gender order is the same: boy-boy-girl-boy.

Another interesting fact is that each of my children have a birthday in a different month. And my wife and I are in two additional months. So, throw in a mother-in-law and a sister-in-law, and we have a birthday in every month of the year (our youngest, Luke, cooperated by arriving 10 days past his due date on April 1… no fooling).

Having kids across a 20 year span can create some interesting juxtapositions. Like carrying around a baby at my son's high school graduation. Or being called "grandpa" more than once. I also distinctly remember thinking, as a young parent of grade school kids, that the way things were going, I was also going to be an old parent. Well, that day has come.

One of my oldest son's best friends is the youngest of six kids. When my son and his friend were 15, I remember once his friend's Dad having to pick up his son at our house.

The Dad must have been in his 50's; when I looked out our window to see if the Dad had arrived, I saw the car in front of our house and the "old guy" fast asleep in the driver's seat. After 20 years of sleep deprivation, I guess you have to catch up while you can.

I think having a lot of kids in this uncertain world is ultimately a sign of optimism, especially now. We kept having children during a period of economic growth and my business grew along with our family. Now, like many people, we struggle with our budget and worry about how we'll get all these kids through college and out into the world. It's a lot harder now raising kids, I believe, and part of that is the recession and being older and part of it is simply the complexity of the world now. From texting to twitter to amber alerts, we require our kids to ingest amazing amounts of knowledge and face much more complex issues as parents than our own did.

But it's still worth it. And a lot of fun.

Jeff Fister, May 2009

THE SECRET OF A BIG FAMILY

I was in Straub's grocery store the other day and someone stopped me to chat. A mother of three, she asked how all of our kids were faring. "I don't know how you do it," she sighed.

My wife and I get that a lot. The truth is — and anyone who grew up in a big family knows this — it's all relative. The harried mother of three at the grocery store isn't unlike the harried father of five at a soccer game or the harried parents of one very curious and active child. Kids' needs expand or contract to fill the space that's available.

So, how do we do it?

The so-called typical American family is one boy and one girl. Parents will say they don't want more than two kids because then they will be outnumbered. There may be some truth to that. But the secret of a big family is that after awhile, the kids start raising each other; they really do help out. It just may not seem like it when our van door opens and they scatter the way roaches do when you turn on a basement light.

But I've found there is a whole other world "down there" among the kids, filled with stern glances and pecking-order authority from the older ones. In fact, if you stay real quiet and let them sort it out, sometimes you can sneak away and take a nap.

Of course, numbers can take their toll. One of our favorite cartoons is of a man crawling up a house-sized pile of laundry, exclaiming, "Dear, when exactly did we decide to have a big family?" There are $400 grocery shopping trips (but never anything "good to eat" for teenagers). There is that one time of day, around 5:30 p.m., when the blood sugar drops all at once and the sound of whining is eclipsed only by the sound of growling stomachs (when I was growing up, when this happened, my parents added another sound: the shaking of martinis).

All families develop their own verbal shorthand to communicate. With so many people wanting so many things at so many times, these phrases can cut right through the babble. I've collected a list of these that we use. Some are meant to be funny, some are meant to just "sum up" a situation between family members. If you're from a big family, some may already be familiar.

You snooze you lose. When it comes to food, kids better be there when it's ready. Sleep in until noon on a Saturday? Sorry, no more cinammon rolls and bacon.

Old yeller. I won't deny it, and you can call family services, but getting five or six independently-minded kids moving the same direction at the same time takes a lot of lung power.

The waiting is the hardest part. "Just a minute." "Wait your turn." "When I'm done." Kids in a big family learn patience; it's rare they get what they want when they want it. This will help them later in life when they deal with the DMV or postal employees.

Be a problem solver. Most kid problems — except for a trip to the E.R. — can be solved by the kid if you, as a parent, ignore them long enough. It's also a great "life skill." Problem-solvers often become successful adults, and even, eventually, move out of their parent's house.

You don't go anywhere quickly. Sometimes I think back fondly when I was single and I could just get up and go somewhere. With our crowd, after you've tied the shoes and put on the coat and yelled at the teenager to hurry up, you're already late.

Getting out of the house. When I leave home, my wife doesn't say: "When will you be back?" She says: "How many are you taking with you?"

"But is there a lot of blood?" You learn to distinguish the cries of real pain or emergency from others. This is the second thing you say after hearing a thud or a scream; the first is, "Is there blood?"

"101 ways to entertain your kids while sitting down." (Dads only). If you finally sit down, you want to stay there. Read a book to a child, even if it's the 100th time for *Dumb Bunnies*. Toss a ball (watch out for the lamp). Have the toddler ride the "horsey" on your knee. Tickle them. Make funny faces. Whatever it takes to keep the kid occupied while you watch the ballgame out of the corner of your eye.

First up, best dressed. With six boys and only five blue blazers, when we're due at a family wedding in an hour, kids learn to grab one that fits… or at least grab one before they're gone.

Family go lightly (FGL for short). My wife does an incredible job cooking for everyone, including our "special diet" kids who don't eat meat (they're vegetarians who don't eat vegetables). But when guests are coming, and something really special is being served, kids learn NOT to take a big portion until the whole table is served.

Pick your battles. This is used a lot with teenagers. As in: "I'm not going to let the long hair bother me. But my 16-year-old son is not going on a road trip to Memphis this weekend with a bunch of girls to see a Phish concert."

Let it unfold. It's 9 a.m. on a Saturday and you have a couple of young kids in the car, a list of errands and a cup of coffee already going cold. After stop number one, a kid asks. "Where are we going next?" Then, "Why are we going there?" Then, "After that where are we going?" Let it unfold, buddy.

Going to the dark side. This is a Star Wars reference to that particular time in a child's life when hormones start erupting and "adolescence" nears. When you will suddenly change from the Honored Parent to the Know-Nothing. Why does this age seem to be getting younger and younger? The good news is that kids really do get older, mature, return from the Dark Side and say shocking things like, "Dad, you're right."

How can we miss you if you never leave? This would be the "flip side" of empty-next syndrome.

All's well. This is what our out-of-town kids are supposed to say first when they call. Before this, a kid might call and start telling you about their weekend trip, dorm party, summer plans and by the way, "I'm in the hospital." Don't bury the lead!

Thanks for the update! This is a gentle reproach for the kid who feels compelled to tell you everything about their day —as they're doing it. Like, "I'm tying my shoes now."

Bubble. A one-word code to an offender which means "get out of my personal space!"

Get along guy. This is what we ask a particularly obstinate four-year-old to be after fighting him at every turn.

A hobby is thisclose to mental disease. Dads just want to have fun, too. From basketball to golf to playing music, or whatever you enjoy, make sure it never takes more than three hours at a time.

Just livin' life. An answer to the eternal "why" questions from toddlers. It's less confrontational than "because I'm the parent and I said so" — and even has a slight Zen quality. As in, "Why do we have to go to the dentist?"

CHICKEN JOURNAL:

FOUR NEW FLUFFY FRIENDS

A few weeks ago, four new living beings entered my house. At least, four new invited residents; that doesn't count all the other creatures that hide in the rafters and shadows of our 1897 house, from seasonal squirrels to mice and bugs.

The guests have settled, for the time, quite comfortably in a box in the basement, with little helpers watching them, feeding them, and cleaning them. I stay mostly on the sidelines, offering encouragement and smiling approval. I haven't been called on to do much (which is my plan.) So who — or what— are these visitors?

We got chickens.

And before you wonder: yes, they're for the eggs, not for dinner. Someone said once you name them, you can't eat them. So, say hello to Fluffy, Scarlette, Chicken Jane, Sam, and Little Jerry Seinfeld.

Our family's adventure in urban poultry raising began long before the Saturday morning in April when my wife and son bought them for $1.50 apiece at Soulard Market. Last year, an article in the *St. Louis Post-Dispatch* extolled the joys of raising chickens in the city. My wife and kids were instantly hooked.

We've had varied experiences with pets. We had a dog named Hershey for a while, a mostly (we think) chocolate Labrador from the Humane Society. Hershey never quite adapted to city life, and loved to bolt free from the house and wander across busy intersections, causing us to drive around in our mini-van looking to snare him home again. Then my son developed asthma problems and the first thing the doctor asked was whether we had a pet in the house. Goodbye, Hershey.

We've also had goldfish bowls and an occasional visit from a school pet, such as the recent Hermit Crab Incident. My sons agreed to take the crabs over spring break. I stayed completely on the sidelines until the morning my sons were supposed to bring them back to school. I was reclining on the couch, waiting for the kids to get ready, when I heard: "Dad, they're gone."

I knew then that I had to get up off the couch, not the least reason being to find out if I had inadvertently sat on the crabs. The cage was just a few feet away on the coffee table.

Luckily, my son found one crab crawling up a bookshelf, and the other turned out to be hidden deep within its own shell just like, well, a hermit.

Anyway, last fall my wife and sons read books, drew chicken coop plans and waited for spring. At that point I was entirely supportive (I even bought a book, *Keep Chickens!* for my wife). And I accompanied my poultry-philes to visit a family in the Compton Hill neighborhood who had chickens. These chicken-keepers seemed normal; they lived in a nice old house in the city like ours and had responsible jobs, and their kids were clean.

Like I said, I decided to be supportive. It's not that I had anything against the concept of chickens. I was just a bit uncertain.

For instance, was it legal? Did we need some kind of permit? What would the neighbors think? (With all of our kids, I already think we're seen by neighbors as the "Clampetts" on the street… then add chickens?)

But I started hearing more and more about the growing popularity of raising chickens. I read another article in the *Post* about a woman in Clayton who has them, and we heard about friends of friends with chickens in Richmond Heights. I searched the Internet and found out that it's a popular new "trend" in Los Angeles; even some movie stars have them.Wow, I thought. Maybe our family is changing from the "Clampetts" to cutting edge.

Lastly, I realized that I could "pluck" a lot of new column ideas from the "fertile ground" of chicken-raising at home. (Not to mention a lot of bad chicken puns.)

SECTION I
But Is There a Lot of Blood? (Childhood Years)

SPECIAL DELIVERY

I cringe whenever I see a sit-com television show depiction of a woman having a baby.

There are common elements: the woman is always screaming in pain while the husband/friend/life partner stands by helplessly as the medical personnel calmly deliver the baby (offscreen, of course). Later, a perfectly pink and clean baby in a blanket is held by the suddenly wafer-thin mom with perfect hair. The husband/friend/life partner stands by, smiling and relieved, looking as if he/she has dodged a bullet.

My wife recently had our seventh child; she's had them in three states and six hospitals. When I think about what I'm good at — what activity I've done repeatedly and learning lessons along the way, other than house painting — I guess I could qualify as an expert in being a "birth partner."

So, in the spirit of sit-coms, I've thought about two characters at opposite ends of the scale in terms of male evolution.

At one end is Ricky Ricardo from the Lucille Ball show. He's a creation of the 1950s, well-meaning but a male Neanderthal — not very evolved. At the other end is Alan Alda, the sensitive star of M*A*S*H. Alda is so evolved that he's practically part of another species.

I've come up with ***actual real-life*** events in my 16 years of "birth experience." What would Ricky do (WWRD) in that situation? What would Alan do (WWAD)? What did I do?

• I'm at a family gathering mid-way through my wife's pregnancy. One of my relatives asks me what we will name the child. WWRD? Puff out his chest and tell the whole room that the child will be called Ricky Jr. (assuming it will be a male child). WWAD? Thoughtfully glance at his wife and say that "We want to wait and find a name that matches the child's karma." What did I do? I said, "We haven't decided yet," even though we had. I've learned: ***never*** discuss the child's name with others before birth.

• I'm at work. My wife calls to say her water has broken. WWRD? Ricky, in the middle of band practice, would coo some reassuring words into the phone and say that he'll meet her at the hospital as soon as practice is finished. Then he'd call Fred to take her to the hospital. WWAD? Alan would have found a job closer to home with built-in "flex time" from his employer. He'd have a pager and cell phone. He'd rush home immediately. What did I do? Like Alan, I rushed home. But it was a 30-minute drive.

• I'm at the hospital with my wife. Labor has started. WWRD? He'd kiss his wife, wish her luck, and go to the waiting room to let the doctors take care of it. He'd smoke cigarettes and pace the room nervously until the doctor-in-scrubs burst into the room with the "good news." Ricky would then start passing out cigars and making excited phone calls for 20 minutes until he was sure that Mom and baby were "cleaned up" and ready to be seen. WWAD? He'd stay with his wife, helping her to relax, to stay comfortable and to breathe with her throughout the contractions. I plead guilty here; I've pretty much turned into Alan on this one.

• Mid-way through labor, a group of OB-GYN medical students walk in. The doctor asks if they "checked" my wife. WWRD? Ricky, faced with a bunch of white coats, agrees readily and bails out of the room, thankful for a chance to have another cigarette. WWAD? He'd say gently, "Is it medically necessary?"

Alan has a point. Beware of overly intrusive doctors and nurses. Hospitals are for sick people; having a baby is natural. You want the doctors and all of their technology around if there is a complication, but much of the poking and prodding is unnecessary.

• My baby has just been born. The doctor asks me if I'd like to cut the cord. WWRD? Ricky, who really didn't want to be "in there" for the *actual birth*, nods "no" emphatically and nearly passes out. WWAD? Alan gently takes the scissors from the doctor, cuts the cord, and asks, "Can I keep it?"

Sorry, Alan, I'm with Ricky on this one. I politely declined the doctor's offer and thought: that's *your* job. That's why I'm paying you good money — well, at least 10% of the actual cost after insurance.

DOCTOR, DO WE HAVE A PROBLEM?

The black and white glow from the small television screen filled the darkened room. As a technician scanned my wife's uterus with high frequency sound waves, we watched the monitor intently as our unborn son wiggled.

This scene is familiar to most modern fathers; a trip to the obstetrician in the early months of pregnancy often requires an "ultrasound," a high-tech procedure in which the doctor can "see" the baby in the mother's womb. But for us, this wasn't early; it was seven months along and the only reason for an ultrasound at this late stage was to check for "problems."

Problems. We had already had three healthy children; the thought — the fear — of a child with a "problem" had occurred to us, but it had never been real.

The ultrasound lasted nearly two hours. The technician quietly scanned and measured the baby's body parts — spine length, head diameter, etc. My wife finally spoke: "Is there a problem?"

The technician coolly replied. "I'm checking measurements against standards. If any deviate, I'll call a doctor in to examine."

"So, if a doctor comes in, there's a problem?"

"If a doctor is called to examine, then measurements might indicate an abnormality. The doctor will evaluate the data."

The technician finally left, leaving a ghostly image of the baby frozen on the screen. After a few more tense minutes, someone else came in.

A doctor.

"Is there a problem, doctor?"

"I was concerned that the extra fluid in your uterus might indicate some kind of heart abnormality," the young doctor replied clinically. "But it's marginal, so I believe it's just extra fluid."

"So there's no problem?"

For a second, her professional demeanor faded. She smiled slightly. "No, I don't think so. Your own doctor can tell you more."

No problem.

WITH SIX, YOU GET EGGROLL (1996)

If someone had told me when I was a kid that I'd have six kids when I was 36, it probably wouldn't have shocked me. After all, growing up in Catholic St. Louis in the 1960s, it was not uncommon for families to have five, six, seven or more kids. Our own family had five.

But now, I still stumble over the words a little when I'm asked socially, "How many kids do you have?" The word "six" sounds almost absurd, and invariably will stop the conversation as the other person gasps. One guy said: "OK, you win."

Or sometimes people will say, "Are you Catholic?" It's a reference, of course, to the stereotype of big Catholic families. Well, yes, we happen to be Catholic and yes, although you didn't ask, we also practice natural family planning. Any other questions?

One of my first thoughts when I learned my wife was pregnant with our sixth child was that we couldn't fit everyone in our mini-van. I'd have to buy a full sized van — or a maybe a bus. For a while, it became almost an obsession. Is there a mini-van that seats eight? I wasn't really comfortable with the thought of buying a huge van that needed a special "truck" license plate. I also flinched when my cousin showed off his $30,000 Suburban; "You can still get a pretty good one for $25K," he said. That much for a car? You can buy a small house in south St. Louis for that.

After a while, it didn't seem to matter as much; we figured we'd just take two cars if we had to go somewhere together.

Besides, a neighbor pointed out, it wouldn't be long until our oldest son (he's 11) wouldn't want to go anywhere with us anyway.

It was in September of 1995 when we learned that my wife, Laura, was pregnant with our sixth child. At the time we were in a bit of shock. We already had a baby not yet a year old. Our other children were spaced two or three years apart. The thought of a newborn and an 18-month old was a bit daunting. We didn't tell anyone for nearly two months — we needed time ourselves to get used to the idea.

One Sunday after church we approached our pastor, Fr. Jim Telthorst of St. Louis Cathedral, to tell him. He came up and said, "Oh, I've been looking for you. I have some news for you both." He said we were to be honored as one of the six archdiocesan "families of the year" at an upcoming ceremony.

There's a saying that goes, "New baby, new house." In 11 years of marriage we have moved five times. So much for that saying — we have six kids.

When I wondered to someone how we could handle all six kids, he just shrugged. "I come from a family of eight kids," he said. "After the fourth kid, the older kids raise them."

Another obsession had to do with having two kids under two in the same house. At the time, my mother-in-law was talking about selling her house and moving into something smaller. I seized on the idea of her building an addition onto our house; she could have her own space but still be around to help care for the kids. I went as far as spending my spare time drawing little floor layouts. We even called an architect, who came to our house and discussed prices and sizes.

Later, I realized how this idea flew in the face of all reality. My mother-in-law has a job and a life of her own; she's a tremendous help as it is. We live in a 100-year-old house in an historic district on a private street — there's no way the covenants would allow an ugly aluminum-siding box to be stuck on the back of our brick house. Thankfully, the idea stalled.

My wife and I probably aren't the best "poster family" for natural family planning. After all (place joke here), we have six kids. You might think we're the result of what happens when people ***don't*** use family planning.

TEETHING: THE BOURBON CURE

I was reminded recently that your kid doesn't have to be an eight-month-old teething baby to wake you up in the middle of the night.

It can also be your 18-year-old almost-grown-up kid who's away at college.

The phone call came early one Saturday morning at 1:30. I answered it groggily and a young woman said "Hi Dan, it's Rachel!" Dan is my son who's a freshman at Truman State.

I started to tell Rachel that Dan was not ***here*** in St. Louis, but in Kirksville, but there was a lot of noise on the woman's end (I doubt she was at the library). She kept calling me Dan, perhaps thinking my son was kidding. I said something about Truman, and she said ***she*** was at Truman. I finally made it very clear that I was Dan's father, I was in St. Louis, and she'd have to figure out some other way to find him. Rachel giggled and then hung up on me.

Meanwhile, not far from where I was sleeping, the phone call awakened my eight-month-old teething baby.

Before I go any further: let me make it clear that any complaints I'm about to make about sleep deprivation PALE in comparison to what my wife is going through. She's a nursing mom and I am the Number One Male Advocate for Nursing Moms (shoot, I'm nearly an honorary nursing mom myself, I support it so much). A mom who nurses her children gets special bonding time with her kids, provides a nutritious start to the baby's life… and her husband doesn't have to get up and feed him.

Anyway, when our baby Luke woke up, this time I did get up to walk with him to calm him down. Since it was the weekend, I didn't have to get up to go to work. During the week, my wife will usually get up with him. That's nice, although I've told her it's not like I'm a ***surgeon*** and I have to be well rested to get up early and save lives. Strong coffee can get me through a day at the office.

Luke's teething had been going on for four weeks and he'd been waking up several times a night. He fooled us for the first six months of life by sleeping through the night. The extended teething period has reminded me: I'm getting too old for this.

Perhaps it's amnesia, or just a middle-aged moment, but I can't remember the other kids teething or how we dealt with it (except for some plastic chewy toys we kept in the freezer). Like childbirth, this "amnesia" is probably a plot by Mother Nature to keep the world populated.

So, we tried many things. Those crumbly crouton-like crackers the baby is supposed to gnaw on. Plastic chewy toys in the freezer. Both infant Tylenol ***and*** little white homeopathic teething pills from the Golden Grocer health food store.

On this particular early morning, I did what any desperate man would do: I broke out the bourbon and thought about rubbing a few drops on the baby's gums — an "old wives tale" cure for teething. Then I realized I probably needed it more; I took a nip and put it away.

Later, in the throes of Luke's restlessness, my wife, the mother of our seven other children, even called a medical professional for advice. "Just let the baby cry for three nights, and then he'll be fine," Nurse Ratchet told my wife. "Who's the boss, anyway?"

Needless to say, in this kinder and gentler era, this suggestion didn't go over too well. It was as if the ghost of Dr. Spock had returned to tell June Cleaver not to worry her pretty little head over it and to just let the baby cry it out. Let's face it: when a baby is screaming in a house full of sleeping kids, he's the boss ***and*** the chairman of the board.

Finally, last week, Luke's teeth broke through. While he's still restless, he seems to be through the worst of the teething. There's a saying that kids are meant to keep their parents up at night; if they don't do it when they're teething babies, just wait until they're teenagers.

As for Dan, he's coming home for Christmas this weekend. Last night on the phone, he asked my wife if he could bring a girl home from school to visit.

That's fine, unless her name is Rachel.

GOT MILK?

I'm a "morning guy." For years I've been getting up early during the school year and shepherding kids off to various institutions of learning.

I wasn't always partial to mornings. Before we had kids I would struggle like everyone else with the alarm clock. But with a house full of kids, I realized that if I get up early, well, it's quiet. And I can have coffee and read the paper without being interrupted. Bingo! Morning Guy.

I'm perfectly happy with this arrangement. In the Ultimate Order of Things at home, my wife at night makes sure the young kids are ready for the next day, laying out their clothes, signing homework, filling out forms and leaving notes. Not to mention that she does the daytime chores of laundering their clothes and grocery shopping. All I have to do each morning is activate the Launch Sequence of making sure six kids get out the door to four different schools. Works for me!

On good days, thanks to my wife's prep work, I can pretty much manage this operation from the comfort of my living room couch. Once I make sure everyone is awake, like a traffic cop I can lay there and yell occasional commands to the grade school kids: "Brush your teeth!" "Put on your shoes!" "Where's your bookbag?" For the teenagers who drive or take a carpool, it's easier: "Don't you need a haircut?"

But to ensure a smooth morning exit (and to keep me on the couch), there are some critical elements of success. Here's my own "Back to School" list:

• **The Number One item above all others: make sure there's enough milk in the house.** My dad, who had five kids, used to joke that we should buy a cow because of all the milk we drank. I agree. Putting milk and cereal in a bowl is a highly efficient way for kids to feed themselves. Otherwise, I'll hear about it. "Dad we're out of milk. Can you make some eggs?" Or: "Dad, there's no bread for toast. What are we going to eat?" Within minutes, the whole operation falls apart. The minutes tick away as I scrounge through the refrigerator. Aha! How about some old chocolate birthday cake? As comedian Bill Cosby said, it *has* to be nutritious. After all, ingredients include milk, flour and eggs.

So even if you have to drive to Schnucks right before bed, or get up extra early to drive to an all-night gas station for a $4 quart of Whole Milk, it's worth it.

• **Automatic Coffee Maker with Timer.** Sure, the Republicans think government is too big, but I think Washington should issue this item to all school parents. When you stumble downstairs at 6:30 a.m. to start the Launch Sequence, there's no better sight than a hot, fresh pot of coffee. Just remember to get it ready the night before (and never use decaf).

• **Keep a clock in view.** Time is relative, Einstein said, and that 45 minutes between waking the kids up and walking out the door can speed faster than a NASCAR race. Periodically checking the clock and yelling out commands is critical. You can finish the sports page later.

• **Delegate responsibility.** Like a good manager, put the oldest and most experienced kid in charge. Let *him* do the yelling for you. Besides, kids listen more to a big brother or sister than their parents.

• **Be ready for the unexpected.** As noted, one thing can cause the whole operation to fail, so be prepared. A kid sleeps late (Keep a headcount. Is someone missing? Since you have to get off the couch, when you get to their room, employ drill sergeant methods to express your displeasure: "I'm not leaving until your feet are on the floor!"). A single tennis shoe can't be found ("Did you look under the couch?" Or: "Can't you wear your brothers'?"). A permission slip is misplaced ("Don't worry, your Mom will find it." That doesn't always work. Sometimes the kid will quiver, cry and insist that he'll be jailed by The Teacher if the slip isn't turned in that very day. So you'll have to write a note, expressing great remorse to The Teacher.) Somebody needs money for a school function. (Since you rarely have any cash, first try reaching under the cushions of the couch. If that fails, borrow from another kid.)

• **Finally, don't ever forget about the milk.** And if a kid says it smells funny, just say it's "fresh." But if the perceptive kid says the expiration date was last year, it looks like you're getting off the couch.

DAD'S DUTIES: SWIMMING & BIKING

With kids out of school for the summer, it reminds me there are only two things I have to teach them in life: how to swim and how to ride a bike.

Unless they can do these, I haven't done my job as a father. This may sound silly, but it's true. *Not* learning these things can cause my kids irreparable harm as they grow older.

Take swimming, for instance. I remember in college when a group of us went to a campus pool on a whim. One girl sat nearby because she never learned how to swim. From then on I never thought of her the same, as if she was stricken with some unmentionable disease. Can't swim? Where was her dad?

So I think: what if one of my kids is grown and is invited to a pool party at the boss' house... and they can't swim? There goes the promotion. What if they're on a honeymoon cruise and fall helplessly into the water? That's the kind of stuff I worry about.

Teaching swimming — whether by yourself or at the "Y" with a group — takes patience. Kids go through stages: no fear of the water at first; screaming fear of the water after the first dunk; and then the creepingly slow progress as they learn to hold their breath, practice strokes and then finally put it all together. There's always the moment when, with pit-of-the stomach-fear, you let go and they swim away, and you pray they stay afloat.

Riding bikes is similar. Though kids seem to be driven everywhere these days, it's still important. One of my sons came home from a friend's house and I asked what he did there. "Well we were going to ride bikes but I don't know how so we just played video games."

Uh-oh. This kid was seven years old and thanks to me, he stayed on the couch playing "Video Doom" instead of going on a bike ride.

The next day we went up to neighborhood playground. I huffed and puffed as I clung to his handlebars. He lurched and veered precariously, barely dodging the tetherball pole. I guess it took some guilt to get *me* off the couch to teach him.

Bike-riding has the same no-fear/much-fear phases. I went through them myself. When my dad taught me how to ride, progress was slow as he jogged along side my bike. One day he just let go and I sailed down a hill, crashing into a bush. I had forgotten how to use the brakes, but at least I stayed on.

Now that I have got teenagers in the house, there is one more thing I have to teach them: how to drive. My oldest son got his learner's permit last week and I handed him the keys to drive home from the DMV. It was white-knuckle time for me, but he did fine. I kind of enjoyed being in a position where he ***had*** to pay attention to what I said.

In a few months, I'll hand him the keys and he'll drive off by himself, another life lesson from Dad. Like the kids pushing away from me in the pool, or my dad releasing his grip on my bike, it's all about letting go.

THE CHILD VEGETARIAN

Autumn in our house brings its own distinctive sounds, from the rumble of soccer kids digging for matching shin guards to the clang of ancient radiators trying to warm up one more time. One of the most dreaded sounds is the pitter patter of tiny feet — attached to squirrels who are seeking the warmth of our third floor.

I've written before about my epic 10-year struggle to keep squirrels out of my house. But when the squirrels returned a week or so ago, it reminded me of something that happened last fall, when my squirrel exploits turned my seven-year-old son into a vegetarian.

He remains one today, along with his older brother.

This happened one evening after dinner. My squirrel-removal routine involves setting traps in the third-floor gutter. When I catch one, I take the animal to my neighbor, who "takes care" of the squirrel .

I usually do my squirrel business late at night after the kids are asleep, but that day I carried an empty trap through the kitchen. My youngest son, Paul, asked me what I was carrying. I explained that it was a squirrel trap. "What do you do with them?" he asked. "I bring them over to our neighbor, and he takes care of them."

Hoping that answer would satisfy his curiosity, I started to leave. "How does he take care of them?" he asked. I started to mumble something and realized that my son probably thought "taking care of them" meant my neighbor brushed their tails and tucked them into bed.

"Well," I stammered…and then my wife came to my rescue. She looked at me and I figured she would create an entirely plausible story which would somehow avoid the unpleasant —but humane — way my neighbor "took care" of the squirrel.

But instead, as I stood there, my wife carefully explained that while we love animals — we have chickens, after all! — when an unwanted critter crosses our threshold and could potentially harm our kids, they have to go. One of our neighbors, in fact, had a squirrel jump out of a desk drawer and lunge at one of her kids.

But as much as my wife tried to explain the "circle of life" to my son, he wasn't buying it. He announced that he was becoming a vegetarian.

I figured it would wear off after a day or two. After all, this was a kid who ate three hotdogs in one sitting and never met a chicken mcnugget he didn't like.

We'd had some experience with this already. My nine-year-old son, Greg, had also become a vegetarian, although it had taken some time. For a while, when he was seven, Greg was on a "modified" vegetarian diet, since he somehow didn't equate a fast-food cheeseburger with meat (I can't blame him).

But he eventually stopped eating any meat, citing his love of animals.

With a household of nine people, having two vegetarians can complicate mealtime. Though we eat our share of fruits and vegetables, we normally have a meat dish every night, and we always need to have something for the "veggies." Let me put it this way: we keep a *lot* of cheese sticks in the refrigerator.

These kids aren't exactly suffering from malnutrition; from French fries and cheese pizza to scrambled eggs and cereal, there's plenty for them to eat.

In the end, it's not a whole lot of trouble, and I respect my young sons for their diet choice (although it got a little tiresome when Paul, as a newly minted vegetarian, would include a sermon at mealtime about the evils of eating meat).

For kids that young to have such strongly held principles, and to stick with them, is laudatory (even if they do go back to eating hot dogs next week). I think it's even caused myself and my family to eat less meat overall, especially red meat. I doubt I'd ever become a vegetarian — or join PETA — but what my young sons are doing has made me more sensitive to the animal kingdom.

Except for squirrels, of course.

DON'T FORGET THE RICOTTA

But where is the ricotta cheese?

It's 10:30 p.m. at the Maplewood Shop & Save, and I'm nearing the end of my 2-hour grocery shopping trip.

Groceries normally aren't on my list of familial duties. Like laundry, this is better done by professionals like my wife. But since last month, when our baby was born, I've done the "big shopping" for my family for three or four weeks.

What's scary is that I'm actually enjoying it. My wife has made it dummy-proof by giving me a detailed list of items, row by grocery row. Her list comes from the "menu planning" she does, a calendar next to the microwave that shows what we'll have for dinner each night for the next month. When you're dealing with 10 people in the house and $300 weekly grocery bills, proper-previous-planning is critical.

One reason I like shopping might be some primitive "hunting and gathering" instinct at work. OK, so I didn't leave the cave and kill a deer with my bare hands to feed my family. But I *did* find the boneless frozen chicken breasts on sale (only three per purchase, please).

Truth be told, it's also nice to get away from the house for awhile, put on headphones, and feel like I'm getting something accomplished. It's good to be moving around on a school night, and bagging my own groceries counts as an upper-body workout.

Also, I'm enjoying it now because I'm getting to know where stuff is. My first trip I spent half my time double-tracking for unfound items. Tonight, I'd done well. I was almost done and only one item was not crossed off my list: the ricotta cheese.

Away from home, shopping gives me time to think. I realize that this spring, more than most, my family has a lot going on. First the arrival of Luke, our baby, on April Fool's Day. My life had gotten pretty predictable in the past few years as our youngest neared five years old. Last year, I'd found time to travel, exercise, read, play in a band and *not* work on the house.

A baby changes everything, of course. What will it be like to be a father at 45 instead of 25 or 35? Let's see, when the baby graduates from high school, I'll be… oh, never mind, I don't do that math anymore. I'm acutely aware of the evening a couple of years (and pounds) ago when a young woman in Borders asked me how old my "granddaughter" was. She was referring to my then two-year old daughter Theresa.

But so far so good; Luke is cooperating and acts as a magnet for the other kids to hang around and even help. Like riding a bike or swimming, I'm finding some of my father instincts coming back – like using diaper pins without drawing blood (mine or his) and that shuffling dance-step called "putting baby to sleep."

At the other end of the kid spectrum, my oldest son is getting ready to go to Europe for a month. He'll spend a week in Paris, and then go to Greece for three weeks as part of an archaeological course through his school, U.M.-St. Louis. I'm proud of the scholarship he got, but probably a little envious, too.

I went abroad when I was his age to visit my future wife, who was studying in France. Probably the next time I'll be able to go back to Europe, if ever, will be as part of some AARP "senior tour" with a chartered bus, daily itinerary and 4 p.m. dinner. But that's OK, at least I had the chance to go when I was young.

My second oldest graduated from C.B.C. high school last week, and there were more mixed emotions. I was proud of his honors and scholarship offers to college, but relieved he wouldn't be driving daily to the large west county campus. I still miss the "old" C.B.C. campus in Clayton, which was convenient for city kids like my son and didn't seem to have quite the snobbishness of a west county private school.

More importantly, his graduation reminded me that in August, we'd have the first kids "leave the nest," another mixed blessing. This summer will probably be the last where we have the whole family sharing regular weekday dinner meals. Maybe that's one reason we had so many kids: it's hard to feel empty nesting when there's a baby around.

Back at Shop & Save, I suddenly heard a voice behind me in the cereal aisle. I turned to see a smiling, nicely dressed African American man with a large gold cross around his neck.

"Excuse me?" I said.

"How's your soul?" the man asked softly.

"My soul? Uh, it's just fine today," I said, a little dazed by his left-field question. "But," I answered, "can you tell me where I can find the ricotta cheese?"

He laughed and pointed to the refrigerated section in the dairy aisle that I'd missed. "God bless," he said as I went to cross off the last item on my list.

CHICKEN JOURNAL:

IT'S THE EGGS

When I was in college, my favorite movie was *Annie Hall*. In one scene, Woody Allen recited the old joke about his brother being so crazy, he thought he was a chicken.

Someone asked why his family went along with it.

"We need the eggs," he said.

When people ask me why we keep four chickens in our backyard in the city, I give a variety of answers, including the fact that we can't have pets in the house because two of my kids are asthmatic.

But as I discovered early in September, there's another reason: we need the eggs.

When my wife and kids brought the feathered friends home in March, they were week-old chicks. The hope was that we'd eventually grow the female hens until they could lay eggs. We had no intention of using the chickens for any other purpose, just as pets. The eggs would be a bonus.

We were told the hens wouldn't lay eggs until they were five or six months old. In late August, I happened to run into an old high school friend, Chris Wimmer, who has an organic farm in St. Charles County. We started talking chickens and Chris asked if we had prepared the nesting box yet.

I had already spent considerable time putting together the chickens' coop for our city backyard. Starting with several wooden contraptions my wife retrieved from the alley, I cobbled together the coop after I made numerous trips to Home Depot and help from my son, James.

But I hadn't prepared a nesting box. Wimmer said that I had better prepare one quickly since the hens were probably getting ready to lay eggs. If there wasn't a separate area for them to lay the eggs, he said, they'd lay them out in the open coop, and the eggs would probably break.

So the next weekend, I put together a nesting box, which was attached to the coop and provided a dark area filled with hay. A few days later, my son ran in the house excitedly, carrying an elongated, rose-colored, double-yolk egg.

Finally, after months of nursing the small chicks in the basement, building a coop, and dutifully feeding and watering them, the chickens had finally produced.

They were paying the rent.

When I e-mailed my sister, she sent back a note: "So, how is your $749 egg?"

The next day the chickens left us a regular-shaped egg, and then nothing for a couple of days. I joked that I needed one more egg for an omelet.

Within a week, we started getting 3 or 4 eggs a day. When I told my father, he said: "That's great, but wouldn't it be easier to just go to Schnucks?"

I was told that "farm fresh eggs" really do taste better, but I'd have to let my kids be the judge. I've yet to taste the backyard eggs, but it's only because of my low-cholesterol diet. When they can create a chicken that produces an "egg beaters" egg, I'll be the first to try it. But I've made numerous omelets for my kids, who claim the back yard eggs taste better than store-bought.

The eggs have come in handy in other ways. One afternoon, my wife was making muffins but realized halfway through the recipe that she needed eggs. She yelled encouragement to the hens in the backyard, and an hour later, she had the eggs she needed.

Woody Allen was right.

SECTION II
First Up, Best Dressed (Big Family Life)

SPRINKLER SUMMER

It's going to be a "sprinkler summer."

I thought about this one day as I was driving home from work. I turned the corner on our street and I had to stop because a group of kids were playing kickball in the street. Three of my own were in the group.

I'd noticed that in the past couple of weeks, kids had been showing up at our door and asking if our kids could come out and, well, just "play."

These weren't "play dates" or parent-supervised activities. It turns out the "play" could range from something as organized as kickball or baseball to riding scooters or to improvising a new game with a tennis racket and a bouncy ball or just hanging out on a brick wall.

Keep in mind, this is not Mayberry circa 1965. It's 2006 on a city street.

Until I was in sixth grade and we moved to a big house on a busy street with no close-by neighbors, I grew up in suburban neighborhoods in Clayton and Tampa, Florida. These were the *Wonder Years* of boyhood, and like the old television show, I was a kid in the 1960s and 1970s, with older brothers and summers empty of school, video games, camps and cares.

My only "job" in those days was to get out of the house as early as possible on a summer morning before my Mom would find something for me to do. I'd wander the neighborhood with friends, walk up to the school playground to play stickball or read a book under a tree. I might stop back home for lunch, but then it was off to the pool and to play outside "until the streetlights came on" or we were called for dinner.

But don't mistake this for some nostalgic longing for days gone by. Kids today have a lot of more opportunities and chances to learn and grow than we did. It just seems refreshing that in this age of fear of crime and over-committed kids, some kids – and parents – are letting go of hectic schedules.

In fact, a recent *USA Today* story reported on residents in a town in California that decreed May 22 as "Family Focus Night."

For the past year, a group of citizens in Poway, California, lobbied leaders of the town's schools, businesses, churches and sports leagues to clear their calendars, so that on the evening of May 22, folks there would be free to do nothing and spend time with their families. This trend, also reflected in books such as *The Over-Scheduled Child* or *In Praise of Slowness*, led one lawyer in Poway to say the activity-free night should give parents "a moment to think about whether they're raising a child or a résumé."

The last couple of summers, we've made an active decision to "slow down" the pace of activities for our kids. First of all, we're fortunate that my wife is able to stay home with the kids. Also, we're lucky that my current group of younger kids aren't necessarily "sports inclined" so we're spared the various baseball schedules and sports camps we'd drag them to.

Inevitably, though, some kid will say "I'm bored. Can we do something fun?" A tradition my wife started years ago during summer is "Wednesday Fun Day." Each week she plans a day of unstructured, free time with the kids that might involve a trip to the Zoo, a picnic at a park or some other for-the-fun-of-it excursion. This serves a couple of purposes — when the kids do have to work around the house, or they say they're bored, my wife can say: just wait until Wednesday.

But we're not completely schedule-free. There is a Cub Scout camp for two of the boys, and my son starting high school wants to try out for the football team, which involves a camp and hot August practices. And we are planning a family vacation to South Carolina like most summers.

Otherwise, the most exciting thing that might happen in a day is when the kids put on their swim suits and turn on the sprinkler. Hey, it's not Six Flags, but they still get wet.

FAMILY DINNER

I remember it clearly. In 1981 I was a senior at St. Louis University. It was late afternoon and I had just finished a meeting at the school newspaper and I had decided to join some friends for pizza at a nearby campus hangout. As a senior, I was quite busy; finishing up school, interviewing for jobs, active in several organizations, I was preparing for life after graduation. While I had lived on campus in my sophomore and junior years, I had moved home for my senior year.

As we ducked into the restaurant, I glanced at my watch. It was 5:30 p.m. and I felt a familiar pang of responsibility. I told my friends I had to make a call and I'd be right with them. I called my mother to tell her I wasn't going to make it home for dinner; I'd be home around 8 p.m. or so.

Even though I was 21 years old and as independent as I could be, I lived at home. And the rule was: if you couldn't make it home for dinner, let your mother know.

I was reminded of this recently when my wife commented about something she'd seen on a morning news program. A "family" expert stated that families should try to eat together as a family at least once a week.

Once a week.

We felt grateful that we'd both grown up in families where the "family dinner" was, well, sacred. Ours was a common scene for a family in the 60s and 70s; we'd have chores before dinner and we'd be seated at a set time. As I remember, when we were younger (I have four brothers and sisters) dinner was quite regimented; we'd have to eat "everything on our plate" before we could be excused. We couldn't talk unless we were recognized, and never with food in our mouths. Invariably my father would ask each of us: "What did you learn in school today?" and I got into the habit of thinking ahead what I'd say.

I remember as a young boy disliking sitting still for the entire time, and also I remember silent and not-so-silent taunts occasionally from my older brothers. Eat everything on my plate? I remember hiding peas under my knife, slipping food to our dog or putting broccoli in my mouth and excusing myself to go to the bathroom.

Sunday dinners were another tradition. That day we'd eat in the dining room at the "big" table with china, and while occasionally we'd miss a weekday dinner together, Sunday was a must-attend.

We always dressed nicely for the feast, and my Mom would make a roast or lamb chops or something special. Even the dinner conversation was upgraded. My Dad went through a phase where he'd have a different kid prepare a report on some topic each Sunday to present to the family.

But, especially as we got older, these were not stuffy, formal affairs. In fact, the conversation would get lively, covering politics, music or — my favorite — old family stories about my Mom or Dad's own upbringing. My Mom was from Jefferson City; my Dad the city kid from Brooklyn.

Now, our family tries to eat together every night, and succeeds at least four or five times a week. Everybody has schedules, so we're not always all there, but the fact we're sitting down together — often with a grandma or a guest — helps complete a day.

As far as conversation… we still have everyone talk about their day. Whether it's oldest to youngest, or "around the table," it's a great way to recognize each person.

But we have some rules. The first one is, never start talking about your day with the phrase, "I got up…" *Everybody gets up* (hopefully). That's because we have a couple of kids who are "linear" talkers, ones who must plod from one event to the next, with no end in sight. So then someone usually yells, "Highlights," which means you have to pick two or three noteworthy events.

But I don't make anyone do a report. At least not yet…

ANOTHER MOUTH TO FEED (AND FOUR MORE LEGS)

I'm a recovering "dog person."

I realized this as I took our new dog, Sadie, for a long walk through Forest Park over the weekend.

Fact is, Sadie and I really haven't bonded yet. It's not that I don't like the dog or I'm indifferent. It's just that Sadie is just one more living thing in my household. And in the hierarchy of who gets my time and affection, there's a long line in front of the dog, including six humans, four chickens and a parakeet.

How Sadie ended up in our home may have something to do with my reluctance.

Last fall, my wife talked about getting a dog for our youngest daughter because she loves animals and she seemed a little lonely since her only sister went off to college.

I remember telling my wife, "I get it." As in: I understand why, at some point, we might acquire a dog. It was the *concept* I got.

But my wife heard me as: "Go get it."

So when my oldest daughter came home from college for Christmas, she, my wife and niece went to the Humane Society. They picked out Sadie, a two-year-old beagle and terrier mix. They arranged to have a family friend keep Sadie until Christmas Eve, when we came home from church and surprised my daughter and the other kids with the new dog.

Sure, I had "concerns." Years ago, we'd had a dog, a large and wild chocolate Labrador who would bolt through the front door and run across city streets. We'd pile into the van and look for her, sometimes spending an hour or more. She was clearly too big and rambunctious for city living, and we eventually found her a better home.

Another concern was our chickens. As regular readers know, we keep chickens in our back yard, four hens who provide eggs for breakfast and another product for our compost pile. From everything I've read, dogs and chickens are not exactly "compatible," given the canine instinct to, um, eat birds. How a dog and four chickens would co-exist peacefully rivaled the challenge of peace in the Middle East.

There were other concerns — extra expense, clutter, etc. — but I saw the writing on the wall. I know when to "pick my battles" and this was not one in which I wanted to engage.

Like the chickens, I found that having Sadie is not as "challenging" as I'd feared. There are definite advantages:

• Sadie is two years old and house trained. This meant no surprises on the carpet in the morning or when we came home after being away for awhile. In fact she's "kennel" trained and sleeps and stays in her little cage when we leave.

• She's small. She's not too big to scare our three year old son and our seven-year-old daughter can walk her without being dragged across the street. Our last dog was very big, hard to control, and had a much bigger cleanup.

• She loves to walk. And so do I, and since she needs to walk every couple of hours or so, that means everybody's getting a lot more exercise in the house. On the walk I referred to earlier, we spent nearly two hours trudging through ice and snow in Forest Park and on city sidewalks and Sadie hardly flinched.

• She's a great conversation piece. I'm suddenly in the world of dog owners, talking with co-workers, neighbors and sometimes total strangers about "all things dog."

• She does her part keeping the house clean by making sure there are no crumbs left on our kitchen or dining room floors.

But the other day I was reminded why we really have Sadie. I was walking in our back staircase and noticed an old framed photo of a miniature poodle. It was a picture of "Shannon," one of the dogs my family had when I was growing up. I remembered that when I moved out of my parent's house after college, my younger sister had gotten a coupon for a free photo of a "family member" from J.C. Penney. To be funny, she brought in Shannon for the photo.

I recalled that when I was nine years old, Shannon was "my" dog and constant companion. Yes, I was once a "dog person" — and now it was my daughter's turn.

THE FAMILY THAT CAMPS TOGETHER

It seemed like a good idea at the time.

On the way to see my parents in South Carolina for our family vacation, we arranged to spend a couple of days with my aunt and uncle in the Smoky Mountains of North Carolina, near Asheville.

My aunt and uncle, who have been retired for years, have a beautiful mountain home in the middle of the Smoky Mountains near Cold Mountain, the peak popularized in the civil war novel of the same name. Having lived near Denver and enjoyed the majesty of the Rocky Montains, I first looked down upon the smokies as a poor substitute. But after having driven through them for the past five or six years, and camped there several times, I've come to appreciate their charm. They are, as my friend Mary Bartley said, the "fuzzy little mountains."

Anyway, not wanting to burden my aunt and uncle with eight guests, we decided that some of us would camp at a nearby campsite and some of the kids would stay with them. We do like to camp, and since hotel rooms would run $70 per night, we figured we'd enjoy the "great outdoors" and save some money.

We found a commercial campsite for $17 a night and reserved it for two nights. The first night, we arrived late, set up camp, and spent an uneventful, if fitful night. A loud mockingbird perched in a tree next to our tent and warbled all night.

The second night, we didn't fare too well. At midnight we awakened to the *plip plop* of raindrops on the top of the tent. The pitter patter increased steadily for about ten minutes and then stopped. We drifted off to sleep then, assuming we'd heard the last of it.

But an hour later, the skies opened and a mini-deluge swamped our tent. I'd been through a couple of these before and knew it was hopeless. Before long we were swimming in water, our clothes soaked, and we grabbed the baby and got into the van. We searched for an hour for a hotel with a vacancy, but it was Fourth of July weekend in the middle of the tourist season and we had little luck. Eschewing the blinking neon light of the "Star Mote "(sic) which advertised "hourly and weekly rates" we finally found a Ramada Hotel at 3:30 a.m. with one room left — a suite for $109 that seemed suspiciously overpriced. Exhausted, we took it.

The next day, on a few hours sleep, I spent most of the morning at the local laundromat as we dried out the sleeping bags and the tent. We finally got back into the car about 2 p.m. for a seven hour trip to our destination.

As we drove along, I did the math and realized we ended up spending about $140 for lodging, the same we would have spent for two nights in a hotel.

But we would have missed the mockingbird.

OH, CHRISTMAS TREE, OH...

I'm a Christmas tree-buying vagabond.

In the 14 years I've lived back in St. Louis, I've been to at least eight different places to buy a tree.

It wasn't always that way. As a kid, each December my Dad would pile the kids into the car and drive a few blocks to the Optimist Club tree lot in Clayton. It was located on Forsyth Boulevard, west of Brentwood, at a site now taken by a skyscraper.

We would walk up and down the aisles of trees, inspecting the balsams and firs. White lights would illuminate the pine-needle path, and the smell of a nearby fire would be pungent in the cold winter air.

My dad would see a tree he liked, pull it out of the rack and spin it around for us. "See any bad sides? Any bare spots?" he'd ask. Eventually, we'd pick one and an Optimist-ic volunteer — usually a business acquaintance of my Dad, a banker — would help us load it into the car.

But since I moved back to St. Louis, I've yet to establish a tree-buying tradition.

I did go back to the Optimist lot once when it was on Forsyth, but at a new location east of Hanley Road. I've rushed last-minute into impersonal stores like Frank's and Home Depot and bought whatever they had left. I've gone the religious route, buying trees at churches like St. Pius V on south Grand Boulevard and a church on McCausland Avenue. One year I traveled to my high school alma mater, Chaminade, and spent 50 bucks on an overpriced fir tree. I went to Ted Drewes two days before Christmas on a cold, rainy day, and brought home a pitiful "Charlie Brown" tree from their nearly depleted stock.

My most memorable tree was the Christmas after we moved into our big old house in the Central West End. With an energy I can hardly fathom today, I had spent all fall furiously removing old wallpaper in the house room by room. Christmas came and we almost decided to forego the tree, as our family and living rooms were torn up and sealed off from the rest of the house with plastic sheeting.

But on Christmas eve afternoon, with a cold, driving snow outside, I trudged up the block with two of my snow-suited kids to New City School, which had an annual tree lot at Waterman and Lake avenues. When I got there, there were only a few trees left, and the workers were closing up for the season. The proprietor urged me to just go ahead and take one, free of charge, but I felt guilty so I gave him five dollars. We then trudged home in the blizzard, dragging the tree, a block-long walk that felt like Admiral Perry's expedition to the North Pole.

It seemed that for whatever reason — price, availability, lots closing down — I couldn't duplicate that tree tradition I had as a kid. I even considered just giving up and buying one of those fake trees that has lights already hung on it. Ten minutes and voila! instant Christmas tree. But when I also realized I'd have to buy a "pine tree in a can" to spray around the family room, I knew that wouldn't work. As a result, tree-buying had become a chore, often done by myself at the last minute.

This past Sunday was to be The Tree Day. I'd put it off, but finally committed when I told the kids first thing in the morning, knowing that they'd bug me all day until we went.

I really didn't know where to go this year. I called Home Depot, and yes, they had plenty of trees. I heard another Ted Drewes commercial on the radio. But then I recalled something a friend, Mary Bartley, had suggested. She said she always went downtown to a place called Glueck's, on north Broadway.

That sounded interesting. I figured I could pile the kids in the van and call it an urban outing.

I avoided the highway and drove downtown on Olive Boulevard. As we entered downtown, I told the kids about another of my childhood Christmas traditions. One night after dinner in December, we'd get ready for bed, put on pajamas, and pile into the back of the station wagon, long before seat belts were required. Dad would drive us downtown and we'd look at all of the department store windows. They were decorated with elaborate displays like robotic waving Santas, miniature train villages, and life-size reindeer. We'd sometimes finish the trip by going to the Anheuser Busch brewery, which each year had a block-long light display. It was our own Winter Wonderland, without the traffic and $20 per carload you get now.

This week, when I got downtown with the kids, I drove by Famous-Barr and was disappointed, but not surprised, to see the display windows barely decorated at all. Most of the old department stores are gone anyway, and with all the renovation downtown, scaffolding was more prevalent than Christmas lights (note to Downtown Now: maybe you should revive the Christmas window tradition. Baby boomers like me would flock downtown again).

We got to Broadway and drove north. We passed a number of old industrial buildings and finally came to Glueck's, which had row after row of trees on an outside lot. We piled out of the car and walked up and down the pine-needle paths. A group of workers were huddled around an outdoor fireplace, and one came over to help us and to give the kids a candy cane. We stayed longer than we had to, pulling trees out of the stands, spinning them around, and finally settled on a long-needle tree that was tall and straight, with not a bare spot to be found. And it only cost $33. When I was paying, the owner said the store had been selling trees for 60 years.

It was late and we had to get going, but instead of taking Highway 40 home, I kept driving down Broadway. "Where are we going?" my son asked, but I didn't answer. Just as I had hoped, I turned right on Arsenal, and drove past the main gates to Anheuser Busch, where the guard waved us through. We drove slowly, marveling at the millions of lights illuminating Busch Place, with towering orange-glowing trees and red-brick palaces outlined with white and green globes.

It felt like a new tradition.

FAMILY "VACATION"?

I wonder if Lewis and Clark had as much trouble packing their boats as my family did loading up for a weekend trip.

On the same day two hundred years ago that the Corps of Discovery launched their boats up the Missouri River to explore the west, we made our own trip up the Missouri to spend the weekend at a farm house near Dutzow.

How could our 21st-century car trip rival the intrepid explorers? Consider this: Lewis and Clark had two boats, six canoes, 31 men, and had to pack supplies for two years. We had three vehicles, 12 people, and had to pack supplies for three days.

But we had six teenagers.

Priorities for the Lewis and Clark trip included food, camping equipment, scientific instruments, tools and guns. What were our priorities? Apparently only one: batteries — and lots of them, in many sizes. God forbid we get stranded without enough power to run the video/computer games and the CD players.

As far as clothing, you may think Lewis and Clark had a lot to deal with, anticipating weather ranging from freezing mountain snowstorms to 100-degree-plus summers. Our intrepid travelers ranged from teenage girls with four satchels each to a teenage boy who decided the only footwear he'd need all weekend were his flip-flops.

There is a phrase I use for a critical moment in the packing process for a family car trip. It comes at a time of maximum stress and exhaustion. You've raced around for two hours, putting stuff in the car and gently reminding (yelling at) the kids to pack their things, to go to the bathroom, and to stop fighting with their siblings.

In that space of two hours, you've faced dozens of on-the-spot momentous decisions, such as: "Dad, can I bring this beanie baby?" (No; there are already 329 in the car.) You've crammed and pushed and rearranged every nook and cranny to make sure everything fits (including a toaster that your wife insists on packing; why not the sink, too?). With the skill of Thomas Jefferson, you've negotiated exactly where everybody will sit in three cars. You've checked and rechecked the list, knowing that about two miles from home, someone will say, "Dad, I forgot all my clothes. Can we go back?" You've even endured the ultimate act of insubordination: a teenager who says you should "Chill out, Dad" as he sits lazily on the porch.

This moment is known as "getting over the hump." At this point, the advantages of leaving or staying are in perfect equilibrium. You're inclined to just walk back into the house, mix a stiff drink, put on the headphones, and take a long nap.

Like Lewis and Clark finally deciding they were ready to shove off, this is the moment of truth.

I have just one piece of advice: always make room for the toaster.

FLOAT TRIP: SHEER TERROR

In early August, I took a float trip with my family. A couple of weeks later, someone asked me how it went.

I struggled to find the words. Finally, I said: "There were long stretches of calm interrupted by moments of sheer terror."

Or, as my three year old daughter said, "It was fun except for the scary parts."

When a family friend suggested the trip, it sounded like a good idea. The friend, Fr. Tom Molini, had baptized three of our kids and was soon leaving St. Louis for a three-month sabbatical in Rome. Hey, what could go wrong if you're floating with a priest? After all, a summer float trip was traditional, like going to a Cardinals' game, Ted Drewes or the Muny.

It had been at least 20 years since my last float trip. It's not that I don't like the outdoors. I love rivers. I love to read about them, watch them, and walk above them on bridges. I just don't necessarily want to be *in* them.

For this trip, we drove to Cuba, Missouri, where we pulled up to "The Rafting Company," a camping and canoeing establishment on the Meramec River. The attendants were pleasant; they took our money and gave us a brochure, and we waited for the bus to pick us up with our sunscreen and coolers. I glanced at the brochure and it talked about parties and food and scenic river vistas. This would be like an afternoon on the Lazy River at Six Flags, right?

We picked a Wednesday for our float. I figured a mid-week excursion would avoid the beer-soaked weekenders I remembered from my last trip. It turned out to be an uncommonly cool August day, overcast and pleasant. There were eight of us: my wife and I, Fr. Molini and five of my kids. We slipped into the water at about 10 a.m., aboard two canoes and one big raft.

I'm not a rookie boatsman; we had canoed and kayaked earlier in the summer in Minnesota and I was pretty confident in my piloting skills. Soon after we started the float, we settled into the easy rhythm of the river. The current swept us gently down the stream, and we watched the green trees and rock outcroppings slide by. Within a half-hour or so, I felt I had left the caffeinated city and cell phone far behind.

Around noon we pulled onto a sandbar and had lunch, a small feast prepared by Fr. Molini, which included deli sandwiches, homegrown tomatoes, chips and soda. After lunch we swam in the river and my son caught a fish. I recall my wife saying: "Maybe we should have brought some beer." Beer, I thought? Who needed beer? I was doing fine relaxing in the great outdoors.

After lunch, I was in the raft with two of my boys, and we hit a long, calm, lake-like stretch of the river. As I learned, the rafts were much more stable, but slower than the canoes. As we drifted slowly down the river, I put my paddle down and stretched out on my back in the raft. For a while I gazed up at the sky, watching a chicken hawk slowly circle high above me. I eventually dozed, the pleasant hum of my kids and the summer cicadas in the background.

Little did I know that *Deliverance* lay just around the next river bend.

About a mile of the five-mile float remained when we switched boats and passengers. My wife and I got in a canoe with our three-year-old daughter in the middle. We glided quickly through a calm part of the river when up ahead it took a sharp turn out of sight. We turned the corner and suddenly we were swept into a swift rapid that shot our canoe directly into the path of an overhanging log.

Within seconds our canoe was stuck under the log. As we sat there, stunned, the canoe started to turn over into the rushing current. It was like a "super-slow-mo" Olympic moment, and I watched as the river dumped my wife and daughter into the river, along with paddles, cushions and everything else in the canoe.

The water wasn't deep, maybe four feet, and with leaden feet I got my footing and plucked my daughter out of the river after she was momentarily dunked, her life preserver doing its job. Together, we trudged to the riverbank, and my wife and daughter sat, soggy but safe, as I surveyed the canoe.

It was wedged under the log, the stream slowly piling up sediment against it.

About ten minutes later, Fr. Molini and the rest of my kids arrived on the raft. For the next half-hour or so, Fr. Molini and I wrestled with the canoe, trying to find the right leverage to free it from the log. Whether it was his strength or heavenly intervention, Fr. Molini finally freed the canoe, and we emerged, bruised but not broken.

We slowly regrouped, boarded the vessels and set forth again, eventually reclaiming the lost paddles, cushions, even my wife's hat, which had snagged on a downstream branch.

As we neared the final quarter mile, we made a final switch of passengers, and I gathered the three youngest kids in the raft. I began to paddle purposefully toward the highway bridge that marked the end of the trip. By this point, I had lost all appreciation of the float trip "journey"; I was ready to get back to civilization.

But as I pointed out, canoes travel much faster, and the others pulled quickly out of sight as I labored in the raft. Then, without warning, a thunderclap exploded above us and within minutes we were caught in the middle of a thunderstorm.

I pulled to the shore, and in the pouring rain dragged my three kids up a muddy embankment and collapsed under a tree. For the next half hour, as the storm raged, we huddled together in the mud, singing hopeful songs ("You Are My Sunshine") and reciting not a few Hail Marys.

In my paranoia about a lightning strike, I looked to remove anything metal and took my nine year old son's pair of glasses off and tossed them behind us.

Finally, the thunder seemed to fade and the rain slowed, and we got back into the raft, not far from the beckoning bridge.

A few hundred yards downriver, my son said: "Dad, where are my glasses?" For an instant, with the end so near, I thought of leaving the glasses. But whether it was fatigue-induced insanity or pride, I decided I had to get them back. After all, we'd survived a capsized canoe with everything intact.

So I turned the raft around, and with both of my boys paddling, we struggled back upstream to our muddy embankment. It was not a small victory when my son ran ashore and held the glasses aloft when he found them in the mud.

I'm not sure how Lewis and Clark felt when they rounded the last bend of the Missouri River after their two-year trek to the Pacific and saw the welcoming crowds of St. Charles. But maybe it was something like I felt when we floated under the bridge, muddy and tired, and saw the rest of our corps waving for us.

Next time I'll bring beer.

T.V.- FREE FAMILY?

I received in the mail the other day two coupons to purchase television "converter boxes" that will enable me to watch television at home after the switch from analog t.v. I'm tempted to put them in the recycling pile.

If, like me, you're one of the 20% of national television viewers who don't have cable or a satellite dish — and still have "rabbit ears" on your old t.v. — your viewing world will end as you know it in June 2009. That's when the federal government has mandated that our old t.v.s will cease to exist and we will enter the brave new world of digital.

If you watch any television at all, it's hard not to know this is happening. Between the "public service announcements," news stories, and the slow crawl across the bottom of the screen, local stations have filled their airwaves with news of the impending change.

Once the big switchover happens, the half-dozen analog sets I have in my house will show only fuzzy static. The options are to get new digital t.v.s, install cable or buy the converter boxes.

But what if I don't participate in this technological "revolution?" What if our family just stops watching it all together?

This would be a good time to quit, at least for myself. I have no "must-see" weekly show like the old *West Wing*. Plus, the election is over so *Saturday Night Live* will become a lot less funny. And, I tell myself, I can watch many shows on my computer — once I figure out how to do that. I would miss some things — live sports, *Donnybrook*, *David Letterman* and *Frontline* — but I could also read a book. Yes, the kids would complain (and it's hard to imagine a world without *Arthur*), but they could still play video games and watch DVDs.

So why the big change, anyway? According to the Federal Communications Commission, Congress mandated the conversion to all-digital television broadcasting, because it will "free up frequencies for public safety communications (such as police, fire, and emergency rescue)." Also, the FCC says, digital is a "more efficient transmission technology that allows broadcast stations to offer improved picture and sound quality, as well as offer more programming options for consumers through multiple broadcast streams (multicasting)." In addition, the FCC website claims, "Some of the freed up frequencies will be used for advanced commercial wireless services for consumers."

Huh? Not to be cynical, but apparently the last sentence of that statement — "freed up frequencies" — is the key. The government will be able to auction off these new frequencies to cell phone companies for billions of dollars so that more teenagers will be able to "text." Woo-hoo!

We did have cable television once. In 1987, when we lived in a new suburb near Denver, we bought "basic" cable for about $40 a month. A year later, we had the same basic channels and the cost was $55. This was before stations like CNN and ESPN had evolved, and I realized then I could still watch the Broncos football team and *Arthur* without the rising cable bill. Would I miss the classic movie channel? Hardly.

When we moved into our century-old house in the Central West End, I called Charter Communications to take the cable *out* of my house. The previous owners had wired every room, bored numerous holes in the historic bricks and it took me a year to finally pull all of the coaxial cable out of the house. When I called Charter to take it away, they tried to sell me on new service.

Since then we've survived with t.v. sets culled from family members, one from an estate sale and even two sets that my dumpster-diving son got from the alley (yes, I checked for bugs). For better reception, I've bought more than a few "rabbit ears" from Radio Shack, applied aluminum foil and once had my son stand and hold onto the antennae during an exciting end to a basketball game ("Right there! Don't move!"). And for some reason I'll never understand (nor want to take to time to find out), we're only a mile from the Fox television tower and we can't get channel 2. Sorry, John Pertzborn.

But could we really live without television? I recently ran into someone who works at a local television station and he told me that if you get a converter box, the picture is a lot clearer and that KETC Channel 9 has four different digital channels.

Really? I said, amazed. I wonder if that means ***Donnybrook*** would be available 24/7.

Hmmm… where *did* I put those coupons?

Brooder lamp	9.00	
red feeder	3.45	
bulb	6.50	
metal feeder	3.95	
thermometer	6.99	
bulb	8.00	
chickens –	10.00	
feed (start + grow)		2.75
" "		2.75
4/27 " "		2.75

CHICKEN JOURNAL:

THE BIRDMAN OF WESTMINSTER PLACE

I recently ran into an old family friend, Jack Davenport, whom I hadn't seen since last summer. "Don't tell me about your kids," he said. "How are the chickens?"

I smiled. That morning, I had gone out to check that the hens had enough food, and hadn't frozen on their perches in the zero-degree weather.

They were fine, comfortably warm with their "down coats" and looking forward, I'm sure, to another day of pecking and clucking.

As you may know, my wife and kids got the chickens last year and I've realized there are some advantages to having four more living things to worry about in our household. Unlike other pets, they actually contribute something — four farm-fresh eggs a day. They also make great conversation pieces at holiday cocktail partiesa. During one pre-Christmas shopping trip to the Bug Store in Kirkwood, I amused two sales clerks and a customer with chicken stories as I paid for a gift for my wife — a "chicken clock."

A recent note from a former neighbor, Penny Chrisler, reminded me that we're not the first family on our block to keep fowl. The original "Birdman of Westminster Place" was Penny's late husband, Tanner Chrisler, who kept and bred 50 pigeons in his garage.

Pigeons are a relatively harmless part of the urban wildlife scene. They're unlike squirrels and rats, which can creep into your house. Or possums that lumber ominously in the alley and crows that form huge black clouds of noise. Pigeons pretty much keep to themselves. They're relatively sedentary until they miraculously fly away from oncoming cars in the street.

Tanner was a pigeon fancier nearly his entire life. In a 1978 article in the *St. Louis Post-Dispatch*, a bemused writer, Jack Rice, described how Tanner not only kept pigeons, but had his own genetics project. Tanner raised King pigeons, one of the largest of the 700 pigeon breeds and two and a half times the size of common pigeons. Tanner was able to breed the normally white King pigeons into a variety of colors. He corresponded with other pigeon breeders throughout the world and occasionally sold several. Some of his rarer birds could fetch up to $500. But like any true hobbyist, Tanner did it for the fun, not the money. "It's not a big thing commercially and I don't want it to be," he told the *Post-Dispatch.* "At the peak of your success you pay for your feed bills."

Tanner also did something we don't do with our birds: he ate them. The King pigeon, because of its size, was bred for the dinner table. On this subject, Chrisler quoted James Beard, who was an authority on "cooking game until it is fit for polite society." In our household, the rule is that if you name them, you can't eat them. So our hens are safe.

A highlight of visiting the Chrisler's house, especially with young children who needed a diversion, was taking them to see the pigeons. Tanner, who had a bunch of his own kids, would patiently show off his birds to rapt children. He'd take them through the pigeon pen, a 10- by 20-foot enclosure with wire mesh and cedar supports.

Our chickens are also a great conversation piece for visitors. Especially when you have unexpected guests with kids and you don't know what to do with them. "Hey, let's go see the chickens!"

Tanner's pigeons were useful in another way; he had the best compost for spring planting. In fact, when Tanner and Penny finally moved out of their big house, an organic farmer and family friend, Chris Wimmer, gladly drove in from his farm in Wentzville to get the pigeon compost.

On this matter I can also relate. People ask us what happens to the chicken droppings? We only have four hens, so every month or so, I move the coop and pen to another spot in the backyard for "natural fertilizer." The grass in those spots comes back *really* green and it saves me a trip to Home Depot for a bag of chemical fertilizer.

There's one more thing Tanner did that I won't have to worry about: breeding. All four chickens are hens, and they've created a nice calm henhouse that a rooster would only disrupt. As my four-year-old daughter might say: girls rule, boys drool.

SECTION III
Going to the Dark Side (Teen Years)

HIGH SCHOOL FLASHBACK (1999)

So, where did you go to high school?

A few weeks ago, I went to the first high school football game I had seen in, oh, 22 years or so. It was the "big game" between St. Louis University High School and Christian Brothers College, better known as CBC. I went because my oldest child, a son, just started high school at SLUH; we decided to make it a family affair.

It was the latest in a series of severe flashbacks I've had since I've re-entered the high school universe.

It began with orientation meeting last spring. I looked around and saw hundreds of boys, some pimply and gawky, others bookish or athletic, and shuddered at some of the more uncomfortable aspects of adolescence.

Like zits. Awkward dealings with girls. "Peer pressure." Uninspiring teachers and boring classes. Taking a shower after gym class in the dead of winter. Bursts of inappropriate laughter.

I've found myself telling my son to "study hard," even though I remember doing most of my homework in the carpool on the way to school or cramming the night before an exam. Apparently that won't work at SLUH; at orientation, counselors told us to expect "two to three hours a night" of homework and studying for our sons.

On the social front, we had to pick our son up after a mixer. Beforehand, I stupidly asked who the band was – "Dad, they don't have bands anymore. Just DJs." That's too bad, I thought. I recalled several mixers I attended with music by Jay Berry, a popular local band in the 1970s. Judging by the noise coming from the mixer, I doubt today's DJs have the song "Color My World" – the ultimate slow dance song – on their list.

But, at the football game we attended, a lot of the "scene" was familiar – the pounding of the pep band drums and the raucous cheerleaders of the two schools inciting their fans.

Afterward, I asked my son how he liked the game, even though SLUH lost to their Clayton rival. "Oh, it was fun," he said. "I had a good time with my friends." And then I realized that some things never change – when I was in high school, I never watched the game either.

ADVENTURES IN TRAFFIC COURT

My 16-year-old son has a lawyer.

When I was 16, I had occasional use of my mother's Country Squire station wagon and a pretty good baseball glove.

While I know a few lawyers I could call in a pinch, I don't even "have" one now.

I found out about my son's attorney when I asked him about his latest speeding ticket. "Dad, don't worry, I've got a lawyer for this one," he shrugged.

"Oh?" I said. "How did that happen?"

"Well, I saw this sign on a telephone pole that said, 'Fix speeding tickets cheap,' so I called him," he said.

I didn't know what I was more shocked about; the fact that my son had a lawyer, or how the guy had advertised (I guess the lower third of the law school class has to work somewhere).

I guess I should be thankful for my son's initiative. After all, it was my wife and I who told him the speeding ticket (his third) was his problem. The previous two, I had referred him to a neighbor lawyer friend and had accompanied him to traffic court in Frontenac.

I'm not a stranger to traffic court.

Between my two teenage sons, I've visited four municipalities in St. Louis county. This is because most cities require 16-year-old violators to have a parent present in court for a moving violation.

The experience is not pleasant. Generally, it involves being herded into a crowded court room. This is followed by waiting an hour or more until a bored part-time judge raises city revenue by banging a gavel and handing out hundred-dollar fines.

Each time, I hoped the experience would shock my sons into slowing down. Maybe it's from watching too much Judge Wopner, but they didn't seem to think it was any different from going to the dentist. Just another appointment to sit through.

When they first got tickets, I would instinctively side with my kids, rationalizing with them that they must have got caught in one of those "speed traps" set up by county police to fund their tree-planting programs.

But that empathy didn't last long. I realized that, trap or not, they were speeding. I remember when you're 16 and you feel immortal, speed limits seem like a real drag. But (worried parent speaking) let's face it: there are a lot more cars on the road and more roads, but a 16-year-old boy's brain hasn't changed. You don't have to be an actuarial genius to figure out that teenage boys aren't necessarily ready to operate a 2-ton hunk of speeding metal. After all, they're beset by raging hormones and a tendency to daydream about girls, jam bands and fast food.

Anyway, it wasn't the Fear of the Law that finally slowed my sons down. It was money. Both sons have to contribute toward insurance and pay their own tickets. When I explained that "points" — unlike basketball — count against you in traffic tickets, they took notice.

My oldest son seems safely beyond the imminent confiscation of his driver's license, and his little brother is learning. After waiting in court for an hour and then forking over 12 hours worth of wages bagging groceries at Straub's, I think (hope?) he's learned his lesson.

The other day, he learned another lesson; he got a bill from "his lawyer." It cost $184 to turn a 78-mile-an-hour cruise through Town & Country into a leaky muffler violation. He was visibly upset, muttering "What a rip-off."

Lesson learned? Maybe he'll decide to go to law school.

GOT THOSE LAPTOP BLUES

Garbage in, garbage out.

That's the old slogan about computers: they are wonderful tools, but they are just tools, only as good as the person using them.

I bring this up because believe it or not, the summer is more than half over and school is fast approaching. Two of the private Catholic high schools my kids will attend next year *require* each student to have a laptop computer. Not just any laptop, but expensive machines with all the bells and whistles you can imagine: wireless internet, DVD players, etc.

At home, we currently have one old 486 Pentium computer with a dial-up modem and a single telephone line. This computer is used by everyone and sits in our high-traffic family room.

I have several problems with my teenagers having new laptop computers for use at school — but not just because they'll have better computers than I have.

First of all, I'm not a technological Luddite; like everyone else, I can't imagine a world without computers. In fact, the computer I'm writing this on — yes, a laptop — is far superior to the room-sized typesetting machine I used 20 years ago when I started my career.

I'm also not a professional educator. I shouldn't presume that I know more about use of computers in school than they do.

The core problem, I think, is that parents and teachers think that just by having computers, kids will be smarter.

I first ran into this years ago when I was on the school board of my kids' elementary school. A new "computer teacher" was hired, money was raised for a "computer room" and before I knew it my kids were spending several hours a week in "computer class." Learning what? How to turn it on?

What real practical knowledge can an eight-year-old learn with a computer that he can't without it? I'd rather have him spending those three hours a week on the "three R's."

No one agreed with me at the time, and part of the problem is that parents don't want to feel their children are being left behind. Simply by saying, "Oh, our school has a computer lab," makes a parent feel like their kid is being properly prepared for our high-tech world.

In fairness to the grade school, they have since made sure that computer classes are integrated into the kids' "real" curriculum; they're learning real stuff with the computers that relates to their real classes.

But the thought of my fourteen- and sixteen-year old lugging around a laptop back and forth from school is scary.

First, it's an expensive piece of equipment. My son last year left his book bag at a city park after lacrosse practice. Needless to say, when we went back to find it, it was long gone, along with several textbooks and (more valuable to him) his CD case of music. What happens if he leaves a shiny new IBM laptop at a football game?

Second, one of the schools next year will have all their students walking around in a new building "wired" for the internet. The idea, the school explained, is that students will go into class, pop open their wireless laptops and start taking notes. The teacher will be able to have materials already loaded on a website for class, and students will be able to access research information instantly.

Sounds good, but remember when you were in high school? I would do anything to distract myself from a boring class. I remember digging small holes into the top of my notebook, drawing an imaginary golf course, and hitting small, balled-up pieces of paper into the golf "holes" and keeping score with a friend across the aisle, all while seeming to pay attention to World History.

Can you imagine a teenage boy with a laptop in class? You think he'll be taking notes? How about playing the latest "matrix" computer game and downloading the newest Phish song (all while seeming to pay attention to World History).

I went to a meeting at the school about the laptops and a friend sat next to me. He works in a big corporate office downtown and his first question was: what happens when the school's network server goes down? "It happens all the time at work," he said. I can see how the teacher will respond. "OK, class, what I'm holding here is called a notebook and a pen. Let me explain how you take notes with these…"

One of the advantages of the laptops, the school said, is that they will eventually replace the need for printed textbooks. My kids now leave the house carrying about 400 pounds worth of books on their back, so putting books on a CD does make sense. But the key word here is "eventually." For now at least, the kids will be carrying all of their books *plus* a 12-pound laptop.

That's the end of my little rant. I have to go now. I have to take the garbage out. Can a computer do that?

KINGSHIGHWAY OF DREAMS?

My fifteen-year-old daughter glanced nervously to her left and then to her right. She gripped the steering wheel of the car, pushed on the accelerator and hesitantly turned for the first time onto Kingshighway Boulevard.

I sat next to her in the passenger seat, and even though it was a quiet Sunday morning, I wanted to take control of the car and let her drive again in, oh, three years or so. Teaching her to drive in Forest Park or in a school parking lot was one thing, but letting her loose on Kingshighway?

I have a love-hate relationship with this road that cuts through my neighborhood and through my driving life. It's mostly hate. In the past ten years, I've had three car accidents; all three were on Kingshighway and none of them were my fault.

One happened when a kid from west county who later said he was lost turned right in front of me. Totalled that car. Another was a couple of months ago when a distracted kid on a cell phone "rear-ended" me as I sat peacefully at a stoplight. The most serious was a few years ago when a S.U.V. ran a red light at Kingshighway and Lindell boulevards, smashed into the back of my car, and then flipped over twice. Luckily in all cases neither I nor anyone with me were hurt.

Kingshighway, legend has it, was named for the King of Spain, who wanted a road that would travel from his post in New Orleans all the way north to St. Louis. I don't know about that, but I do know it has become one of the city's busiest — and most dangerous— thoroughfares.

Between Delmar Boulevard and highway 40/I-64, the Kingshighway "speedway" has three lanes in each direction and 10 stoplights in a mile-and-a-half stretch. At any given moment, you can encounter emergency vehicles racing to or from Barnes Hospital and speeding drivers ignoring stoplights. You can also face traffic tie-ups around the Chase Park-Plaza, wandering joggers trying to get to Forest Park and (my personal favorite) aimless vehicles from St. Louis county making sudden stops or turns for no apparent reason.

A couple of years ago, when I drove my kids to school, I started writing down license plates of cars who ran the stoplight at Waterman Avenue and Kingshighway. In a month I had a list of about 40 cars. I sent the list to the police and talked to a nice captain who said they'd put a traffic car at the light for awhile, but he couldn't do anything about the list I sent him. Though I grudgingly understood that the police have a multitude of urban crime priorities, I wanted those drivers in *jail*! I even fantasized about slapping a fake police light on top of my car and trying to make a "citizen's arrest."

Recently, I've been observing Kingshighway from another perspective: as a pedestrian. In August, I started walking the three blocks to work I normally drove, and each day I'm greeted "up close" with the deafening noise and smoke coming from the road. I've also understood better where walkers exist on the vehicular pecking order — right down there with "road kill." I've stared down more than one driver who tried to run a red light as I was crossing. I've felt a kinship with the legion of bus riders who must wait patiently in all seasons for their Kingshighway ride. And I've been greeted with the bizarre experience of a "talking car" — a prankster who tried to get my attention by talking to me through his car loudspeaker.

I was talking about this recently with a neighbor. He said his wife has had numerous fender benders and he's decided he will not drive on Kingshighway at all anymore. "It can be done," he said, as I eyed him disbelievingly.

It made me think. While I could never make such a change myself, I could do one thing — keep my daughter from driving until she's 18. It can be done.

I WANT YOU... FOR SELECTIVE SERVICE

I'm headed for the nearest foreign border
Vancouver might just be my kind of town
'cause I don't need the kind of law and order
that tends to keep a good man underground
- The Byrds

As I rifled through the day's mail at home, I almost passed the innocuous-looking direct mail piece addressed to my son. But two words caught my eye: "selective service."

Whoa.

Two days after I got the mail, my oldest son turned 18. The flyer was addressed to him with his social security number and a perky little message that said, "It's easy! Register by e-mail or by telephone!"

On first glance it could have been any kind of junk mail offer, selling a cruise, a new credit card or, for my son, another solicitation from a college.

But this offer had a catch in the small print: "Failure to register is a felony and punishable by a fine of up to $250,000 or 5 years in prison."

Selective Service, of course, is the harmless-sounding invitation by the U.S. Government to be available to be drafted. If you're a parent, though, it's also the possibility of your son being sent overseas to maim and kill (or to be killed) on foreign soil.

With storm clouds gathering over Iraq, and a president seeming too-eager to plunge into a war in the tinderbox of the Middle East, the notice to my son gave me pause.

I say that, of course, as part of an ever-older generation who has never served in the armed forces or even been threatened to be drafted. The Vietnam War draft ended in the early 1970s and young men ever since have not had to face the prospect of unwanted military service.

It's easy to be against a draft when you're safely beyond the age where it might include you. It's also easy to fall into the romanticism of the 1960s anti-Vietnam War crusade.

I was in my early teens when the Vietnam War ended but because of my older brothers and my interest in music, I quickly adopted the prevailing anti-war mood. I listened to the albums by Bob Dylan and Crosby, Stills & Nash and I read about the Free Speech Movement and the Chicago Seven. I almost wished I was able to participate in anti-war demonstrations. I used to think I'd make a good "hippie" — but I was too young. Really, I was just a wanna-be from the suburbs going through teenage rebellion.

My wife and I joked with my son about "going to Canada" if he was ever drafted. I realized that this was an almost instinctive protective parental response. The truth is, my son is still pretty far from being called into a war. The draft would have to be reinstated, and the issue of being a college student or not would have to be resolved.

But if he or any of my other four sons were drafted some day, I wouldn't like it, but I'd probably tell them to cooperate — unless the war was completely unjustified. Jimmy Carter said recently that all war is unjust; maybe it is if you're trying to impose your system on another country (Vietnam) or you want to protect economic interests (oil). But what if the war is to protect your own country or to oppose a legitimately evil threat abroad? It may sound trite, but we owe our privileged way of life to the soldiers who have fought and died in such wars. I had a grandfather who fought in World War I and two uncles who served during peacetime. In countries such as Israel, which live in the "lap of war," young people are required to do military service. For the large majority, they serve their time and then get on with their lives. Two years to help ensure a way of life seems reasonable; again, I say that knowing that *I* didn't have to do it.

A few days after my son got his selective service notice, I asked him if he'd registered yet. He looked at me a little puzzled and said, in a typical "whatever" teenage attitude, "Oh, was that something I was supposed to do?"

I was tempted to say, "Naw, just forget it" but I didn't.

"Yes, but it's easy," I said. "You can register by email."

SCHOOL OF ROCK

I went to Blueberry Hill in the University City Loop last week to see a concert. There were a series of rock bands playing a mix of "cover" songs and originals in the basement club known as the Duck Room.

The last band was called "Open 'Til One." They ended with a cover of the Ray Charles song, *What You Say,* including solos by band members and a fun call-and-response with the audience.

I took a particular interest in the tall young woman playing electric bass. She adopted a cool-but-uninterested "look" and occasionally flashed a big smile.

That smile is very familiar to me. It's the same one I've seen in my house for the past 16 years — the smile of my oldest daughter.

Most parents might shudder at the thought of their child playing rock 'n roll in a smoky nightclub. Body piercings, tattoos, mosh pits and green-haired Mohawks might come to mind.

But on this day, they served only root beer at the bar, and the audience was filled with parents, grandparents, friends and little siblings of the band members. It was a concert put on by Dave Simon's Rock School, which teaches kids how to play in a rock band. The concert was, as my wife said, a music "recital" for the new millennium.

The last recital I'd attended for my daughter was in a grade school gym in south St. Louis. Since she was in third grade, my daughter has been taking weekly piano lessons from a nice older nun at a parish grade school. At those recitals, a stream of dressed-up kids would nervously announce their recital pieces into a microphone before an audience of family members sitting in folding chairs. The selections included a mix of Mel-Bay music book classics, ranging from *Candyman* to *Canon in D*. The catchiest song I ever heard was *Red River Valley*, not exactly a toe-tapper. But the piano lessons gave her a solid musical background.

The rock school was my daughter's idea. Some clever direct mailer sent her a postcard about Dave Simon. A few months earlier she had bought herself an electric bass but had trouble organizing a "jam session" with other music-loving friends.

I was a little skeptical at first. I'd seen the movie *School of Rock* where actor Jack Black played a lowlife rock musician who eventually finds salvation teaching kids rock music at an uptight private school.

Dave Simon is no lowlife. We first met with him at his school, located in a modern office/studio in a business park in Olivette. The clean-shaven young man exuded none of the phony enthusiasm of an aging hipster trying to be "cool" for the young kids. He was a good teacher, had solid musical knowledge and an organized system. He explained that kids first took traditional one-on-one lessons with instructors and then eventually "graduated" to playing with others in a band setting.

At the concert, most of the kids seemed like my daughter — clean-cut, musically talented, but anxious to have fun and try out this "rock band" thing. Ranging in age from pre-teens (the "Junior Mints") playing three-chord rock oldies to high school kids playing modern-rock original songs, I didn't see any nose rings or exposed bellies. About as radical as it got was one bored-looking girl who wore a shirt that read "boys stink."

Of course, I'm somewhat to blame for all of this. Four years ago I got a call from an old high school friend who asked if I wanted to "jam" with him and some other guys. Thus started my middle-aged journey back to playing music with friends. We eventually formed a band and started playing at church festivals, private parties and various basements in south county. In fact, the same night as my daughter's Rock School concert, we were playing a St. Patrick's day party in Overland (shameless self promotion: the name of our band is Maxx Roby — remember the old newscaster? — and we play blues and classic rock mostly for fun, beer and occasionally some money).

Is this my mid-life crisis? Maybe, but for me it was a lot more fun than golf and cheaper than a sports car. Also more inspiring — although my wife might disagree.

One result of my "geezer band" pastime was that it suddenly became permissible for my kids to start playing music — and for me to buy more musical instruments. It started with pawn shop electric guitars and keyboards and eventually led to a P.A. system, drum set and a "music room" on our third floor where kids (and Dad) can turn it up and, well, "rock out." In fact it's hard to walk through our house without tripping over some kind of stringed instrument.

With all of this budding musical talent, people joke about us having a family band like the "Partridge Family." Actually, only once or twice have we all tried to play together. Various kids play with each other, but I decided when this started I wouldn't be the overbearing music parent. I wanted to make sure it was fun and not something else Dad was yelling at them to do.

Still, at the concert, it was strange watching my daughter on the same stage where Chuck Berry plays every month. It's hard enough realizing your little girl is growing up, but to see her playing in a rock band with four guys around her was thrilling but a little bit scary. What was I encouraging here?

But then I thought — it's hard to find a good bass player, and if my band ever needs one…

SENIOR SKIP DAY: CLIMB EVERY MOUNTAIN?

News Item: *Why? Because there are no mountains around, two high school seniors told arresting officers Tuesday after climbing to near the top of the University Club Tower, across Brentwood Boulevard from the Galleria in Richmond Heights. Firefighters stood by with ladders and rescue gear, but the teens came down the 23-story structure on their own, unhurt. Police identified the two as Jack McKinney and Tom Slattery, both 18-year-old seniors at Chaminade College Preparatory School in Creve Coeur who did the stunt as part of "senior skip day" at the school.*

From the St. Louis Post-Dispatch *and television reports*

In 1977, I was an eighteen-year-old senior at Chaminade High School. One Wednesday evening at home I got a phone call from someone in my class.

"Tomorrow's the day," he said in a conspiratorial tone. "We show up, then everybody leaves for [name withheld] house."

Things were already edgy at home. My mom had confronted me with a letter she'd received from school that day alerting parents that seniors were planning a skip day on Friday and promising all kinds of consequences if I didn't show up.

Senior skip day had become something of a tradition at the school, but it was always secretly planned, never endorsed, and had always caught school administrators by surprise. A small group in our class had been planning a particular Friday for the skip day.

This particular year, somehow the administration had found out and had sent out the letter to thwart the planned day.

What the school didn't count on was a student who heard about the letter at school. And in a late-period social studies class that day, with the winking approval of the teacher, Mr. Czarnecki, a senior pulled out a school buzz book. He tore out pages of senior phone numbers, and passed them out. "Call everybody tonight. We're going tomorrow, not Friday."

The next day, I did show up at school with carpool but instead of walking out, I decided to go to one class. It was an off-campus "social service" project. A friend and I were volunteering at the nearby Ranken Jordan home for disabled children. I felt nobler that I at least went to that class.

My friend and I then headed over to [name withheld]'s house, whose parents were gone. [Name withheld], a 19-year-old senior, drove over to Illinois, where he could legally buy "3.2" beer (the lower-alcohol beer allowed at the time). The rest of the day we ate pizza, threw a Frisbee around, dozed in the sun and played Allman Brothers Band records (the 33rpm kind) very loud.

I hitchhiked home late that afternoon to confront my parents and my fate, which ended up being a one-day "in school suspension" on a Saturday, working in the school's garden and cleaning bathrooms.

Turns out, after our skip day, the school, tired of the annual disruption, officially instituted a "senior skip day" on the school calendar the next year. What fun is that?

It was this scheduled skip day that the two Chaminade seniors used to climb the U. Club Tower last week. Other than the name of the day, our two events had little in common.

First, none of us — at least that I know of — thought of getting mountain climbing equipment and scaling a skyscraper. Climbing the rope ladder in gym class is about as daring as we got.

No one spent the night in jail for our prank. There was talk that police showed up at [name withheld]'s house later, but I had gotten out of there so I'd be home for dinner. (Although many of us spent quite a few more weekend evenings grounded at home.)

None of us had any intention of getting our prank on television or threatening our impending graduation. It was simply our way to thumb our noses at the administration in our last semester.

On the other hand, it's doubtful that any of the Chaminade seniors this year spent the day at someone's house having a party. First, absent parents now can be prosecuted for that. And with cell phones, it's a lot easier to keep track of your kid. And I would guess that most seniors at Chaminade these days drive themselves to school and NO ONE hitchhikes to get around like I did.

But that said, there's one thing I can identify with regarding the building-climbing incident. On the 10 o'clock news, they showed a glimpse of the father of one of the kids walking into the police station.

The look on his face… well, I've seen that look before. As the father of teenage boys, I've even worn it a couple of times. I made a mental note: check the basement for any mountain climbing equipment.

IT'S TIME TO ACT

On a recent Saturday morning I found myself alone at the confluence of the Mississippi and Missouri rivers. At dinner that night I told my family about it; I said I could have stuck one hand in each of the rivers.

Someone said: "Why would you want to do that?" Ha-ha. Because it's *there,* I wanted to tell the little comedian.

Sitting on the rock at the tip of the confluence park, I could have thought about the beginning and end of the Lewis & Clark mission. They had passed this confluence going out and back from their journey. But instead I thought about why I was lucky enough to be by myself on a busy Saturday morning in September. With soccer games and music lessons and dance lessons to take my kids to, I had been granted the choice Kid Errand: I drove my 17-year-old daughter to Alton High School in Illinois so she could take her *third* ACT test for college.

For me, this was a novelty: a kid who was organized, prepared and ambitious about going to college. Straight-A grades, high school activities, AP courses and college visits — I had run into a creature from another planet. In other words, *not* a high school boy.

My two oldest sons are in college now, but when they were seniors in high school, they weren't exactly worried about the next phase of their lives. I had to bribe my oldest son to get out of bed in April of his senior year to even take *one* ACT.

The second kid was a little more motivated, but more interested in the road trip he and his buddies had planned after graduation than where he'd go in the fall. In the end both applied and were accepted to one state school (UMSL and Truman), and are actually doing fine.

I can relate. When I was a high school senior, my dad was a professor and administrator at St. Louis University, so I knew where I was going because tuition was free. I took the SAT because I had to, and only applied to SLU. Had I had any ambition, I could have applied to another

Jesuit university like Georgetown, but that would have taken too much trouble. So I went to SLU and I did fine.

My daughter is in another world, and I'm not quite sure how to handle it. Since she is ambitious and does have good grades, she will have more options than her brothers. The problem I face, like any parent of college-bound kids, is economic.

"What if your kid wants to go to a $40,000-a-year private school, and after all the financial aid and scholarships, there's still $10,000 left? How can I tell them to borrow $40,000 to get a history degree?"

Those are the questions I posed one night to two Washington University admissions counselors at a "college night" at my daughter's high school. After scholarships, student loans, student work study and some help from my parents, the net cost of both of my sons' tuition is a couple of thousand dollars a year.

But my daughter? She'll figure it out. After all, she's not a boy.

WHITE DADS CAN'T DANCE

It was after 11 p.m. in Khorassan Room at the Chase Park Plaza when the Bob Kuban Band started a of medley of disco hits from the 1970s. That's when I had a keen sense of the passage of time: how old I felt and how mature my 15-year-old daughter looked.

The occasion was a father-daughter dance for my daughter's all-girl high school, Visitation Academy. Earlier in the evening, before going out, a friend had called me. He is a transplanted Chicagoan and suburban dweller. I told him what I was doing that night and he said, "Oh, is it one of those Catholic things?"

I guess it is. I remember years ago my dad taking my sisters to a Father-Daughter dance. Of course, my dad could actually dance (and still does). I have adopted the middle-aged-white-guy shuffle. This is a herky-jerky style which elicited a few Dad-you're-embarassing-me looks from my daughter. Truth is, 25 years ago I danced to *Brickhouse* in the same way, no doubt embarrassing the girls then, too. At least I didn't suggest the "bump" at my daughter's dance.

In some ways, the evening was a high-school flashback for me. Like a prom dance, I gave my daughter flowers (that my wife bought) and we stood for pictures in the living room. When we got to the Chase, my daughter soon disappeared with her friends to giggle and drink soda while I stood around with other dads who were probably thinking the same thing I was: what happened to my little girl? (Yes, I liked the movie, *Father of the Bride*.) Later, the girls dutifully danced with their dads, and then they danced with their friends as we gasped for air and rested at the table.

The night before, I was downtown at the Millenium Hotel for a father-son dinner with my 17-year-old son (no dancing required). He goes to an all-boy high school, C.B.C. Yes, another "Catholic thing."

I vaguely remember going to a Father-Son dinner with my Dad. I'm sure I was thinking then what my own son was probably thinking the other night: "Can I have two desserts?" My Dad back then probably was thinking what I was last week: "Will this guy ever stop talking?"

Like the dance with my daughter, it was a chance to see my son dressed up and with his friends, acting like a socially responsible adult. All cleaned up, he looked less like the slouching, sleeping-late, tie-dye-shirt-wearing teenager I berated than the young man he has become.

The cocktail hour at my son's event was loud and crowded. The high school jazz band was playing, and the room was filled with paunchy-looking guys talking about sports, business, and if they were alumni, about old high school football games.

Continuing the theme, the guest speaker was a local television sports anchor. The broadcaster, also an alumnus, took good-natured jabs at the school's faculty and told self-deprecating stories of his own high school experience. He finished with a few "behind the scenes" tales of local sports heroes.

At the table, we talked about "man" things like, well, sports — how about them Rams? Sports are safe; it's a universal topic among guys who don't know each other and who aren't sure of each other's political bent.

One good thing about the evening was that the school invited grandfathers or other family members to attend. My own Dad was out of town so I asked my brother, Rick Fister, to go with us.The food was OK, the speaker was so-so, but it was nice to visit with my brother and to look at my all-cleaned-up son.

And I didn't have to dance to *Saturday Night Fever* two nights in a row.

CALIFORNIA, HERE SHE COMES

I remember reading a cartoon showing two mother hens in a barn. One says to the other: "I've had more than 600 eggs and not one of them writes or calls."

"Empty nest." Now there's a stage of life I don't worry about. Perhaps that's why we had so many kids. By the time the last one leaves, I'll be too tired to notice. Or others will be moving back in.

Still, two recent events brought this issue home to me.

Last weekend, my oldest child, a son, graduated from Kirkwood High School.

For my wife and me, this was *huge.*

I barely remember my own graduation. But the fact that my first kid, and the first grandchild on either side of our families, graduated, was a big deal. It may also have to do with the difficulties he had early in his high school career — us wondering if he would *ever* graduate as he navigated the turbulent waters of adolescence and we learned to deal with our first teenager.

After first deciding to go to the University of Missouri at Columbia, my son recently decided to go to University of Missouri St. Louis, and stay at home for at least next year. It was a practical, grown-up decision. We were perfectly willing to borrow money for him to go away to school, but he said he wasn't sure what he wanted to do, and he might as well save the money and get some requirements out of the way at UMSL. If he liked it, he might stay.

But even though he's not physically moving out yet, it won't be long, and the high school graduation milestone was another step to adulthood.

The other event happened a couple of months ago. For her spring break, my 14-year-old daughter got on a plane by herself and flew to see my sister in Los Angeles.

That might not seem like a big deal; it wasn't, at first, for me, when I made the plane reservation in February. It was my idea; plane flights were cheap and I wanted to reward her for doing well in school.

But as the departure date drew near, I began to fret. What was I thinking? At the time, the U.S. had just started the war, and as troops got nearer to Baghdad, I realized both she and the troops would be arriving at their destination at the same time. What was I doing, sending her to LAX, Terror Target Number One?

I had major Dad-panic. I called the airlines to see if I could re-route the flight to the Burbank airport, because surely the terrorists didn't care about Burbank. While they were nice at Southwest Airlines, they couldn't change her destination, but at least they put her on a direct flight for her return.

The day she left, I took her to the airport two hours early and I helped her through all the security check points. Luckily, they let me accompany her to the gate, and when we got past security I realized we had nearly an hour and a half to wait. More time for me to worry and to watch CNN to get the latest update on troop movements.

Fortunately, I ran into a family friend, Tim Dorsey, who travels all the time and was in the airport for a flight to Baltimore. He sat with us at Burger King and we had a great time visiting and looking at pictures of his new twin granddaughters. He was so blasé about traveling, it seemed silly for me to worry so much.

Before I knew it, it was time for her to board the plane. I stayed with my daughter all the way through boarding. I would have asked to get on the plane and interrogate all the passengers for potential terrorist tendencies, but even I knew that was a bit much.

I stood there and watched my daughter walk down the ramp to the airplane and I was surprised how old, how mature, how, well… *grown-up* she looked.

I hope they write and call.

GOING TO THE DARK SIDE

When my wife and I were going through some "troubled teen" years with a couple of our kids, another parent told us: don't worry, they'll come around.

I'm here to say — older and grayer — that's true.

What happens when a child turns one day from a sweet, loving kid who does what you say into a surly, sneaky alien who thinks you don't know anything? What happens when a straight-A kid suddenly is getting suspended from school? Hormones happen, that's what.

Here are some things we've learned over the years with teenagers.

Call the Parents. If your child says they're going to a party and the "parents will be there," go ahead and call the house. This isn't necessarily a question of trusting your kid; it's knowing that adolescents may not always make the best choices. As one former U.S. president said about negotiating with Russia during the Cold War: "Trust but verify."

Once I called one of my sons on his cell phone, and heard loud noises in the background. "Are the parents there?" I asked. "Sure, Dad." "Well let me talk to them." Pause. My son then apparently didn't know how to cover up the receiver of the phone and I head him say, "Hey Joey, my Dad's on the phone, talk to him and sound like your Dad." So it may be a little uncomfortable to call a parent, but even if you don't know them, it tells your kid — and the parents — that someone has checked.

Cell phones themselves can be troublesome, because unless you have a GPS receiver in the phone and NASA technology, you don't necessarily know where your child is. Sure, you can *talk* to them, but, well, see above.

We haven't allowed our children to have their own cell phones until they were at least seniors in high school. While phones have become nearly ubiquitous, and grade schoolers are texting each other, it's expensive when you have a lot of kids. And as the kids get older, I think they've come to appreciate it… unlike their friends, they can't be bothered night and day by others. We've gotten around the safety issue by letting them borrow one of our cell phones when they go out at night.

Yes, you can search your child's room. As far as I know, the Constitution's right to privacy doesn't extend to your own 14-year-old. While kids might seem older and more mature these days, they're still kids. The dangers of drugs and alcohol are very real, and suspicion alone is "probable cause" to search their room and belongings. Also we've never allowed our kids to have a lock on their bedroom door or allowed a television or computer in their rooms. I know it's been well documented, but it really is true: computers should be out in the open and viewable at any time by parents.

There is no stigma about meeting with a psychologist. If you're having trouble with a kid, don't be afraid to see a professional therapist. We've had the best luck with psychologists (the "talkers") who specialize in teens. Sometimes the problems get too big for the parents to handle and having a third-party disinterested professional can really help. And often it's the *parent* who needs the help to understand what's going on.

Both alcoholism and depression have appeared on both sides of our family, and as much as you might not want to admit it, it's important to recognize the signs of adolescent trouble. Wondering why your good little boy or girl is suddenly getting kicked out of school, and worrying about how that "looks" to your friends, isn't helping your kid.

Medication isn't always the answer, either. Psychiatrists can prescribe powerful drugs — and many are life-savers — but be sure to also explore therapy.

There is no "bad" time to talk to your teen. Adolescents are trying to figure out their place in the world and often they don't want your opinion. But part of the deal of signing on to be a parent is that when your teens are ready to talk, you should be ready to listen. This could be at 2 a.m., in the middle of watching the World Series or right before you're ready to go out for dinner. While there are many times you need to talk to your child and they're not ready to listen — after you open their report card, while you're driving them to the movies — it's when *they* want to talk that it's most useful.

Oh, and you might as well face it: you'll never, ever get enough sleep.

CHICKEN JOURNAL:

TROUBLE IN THE HENHOUSE: A TALE OF TWO ROOSTERS

"Little Jerry Seinfeld" has gone to a better place.

That's the name my oldest son gave one of the five chicks my wife brought home from Soulard Market in March.

My oldest son — who can find a reference to ***Seinfeld*** or ***The Simpsons*** for every situation in life — named the chicken after a Seinfeld show. In the episode, Jerry's hyperkinetic neighbor Kramer brings a chicken home to his apartment, hoping to get eggs. It turns out the chicken is a rooster, not an egg-laying hen, and the bird's early-morning crows upset the whole apartment building.

So when our kids were naming the chickens, my son chose Jerry as his own. It turns out, like the episode, Jerry *was* a rooster. His days were numbered.

When my wife was researching raising chickens, she learned that gender selection of chicks is an inexact science, and even though you think you're buying hens, invariably a few roosters sneak in (I don't really want to know how you can tell one from the other).

Unless you want to breed chickens, or you plan to have them for Sunday dinner, it's generally a bad idea to keep roosters with hens. Roosters get bigger and more aggressive than the "gentler sex" (oh,those *men*) and can cause henhouse problems. Not to mention problems with neighbors when the roosters start their daybreak "cock-a-doodle-dos."

There's another reason not to keep roosters: The Law.

My wife learned that in the city of St. Louis, residents are only allowed four chickens per household and roosters are forbidden (is this sex discrimination?). The law must be an old one, written when rural people flocked to the big city with their chickens.

So all these factors conspired to send Jerry away. We decided to wait until he had grown, and within a few months, he was sporting a bright red comb. Like the research said, he didn't play well with the others; he grew bigger and bossier than the docile hens. Finally, when his tiny squeaks turned into almost full-throated crows, we knew it was time.

But where could we bring him? One friend said his parents lived on a farm in Washington, Missouri. While that sounded good, the friend cautioned us: "sure, you can bring him out there, but don't expect to visit him." In other words, Jerry would end up on the dinner table. Given our kids' attachment to Jerry, that really wasn't an option. Remember: once you name them, you can't eat them.

Then we found out that one of my wife's friends owns a farm in House Springs. They needed a rooster for breeding, so one recent Saturday morning, we packed up Jerry in a couple of laundry baskets taped together and drove out there with the kids.

Any fears of separation anxiety vanished when we arrived at the farm. I'm a city person, and when you say "farm" and "House Springs," I envision old cars in the front yard, animals running wild, barefoot children and, well, overalls.

But the farm was a lovely place, with a modern home nestled in green hills. The barn was a large, dry, airy, clean building. In a corner was a room-sized chicken pen, complete with lighting, straw floor, and plenty of food and water. There were a bunch of chickens, but they all had plenty of space. And when they wanted to go outside, they were free to roam across a large nearby field.

This compared to the relatively cramped quarters Jerry shared with the hens in our homemade backyard chicken coop. So much for city living.

We put Jerry down in the midst of his new family and within a few minutes he was clucking happily. (We later learned that he had to be separated from the hens because he was larger and older, and he had quickly put himself at the top of the "pecking order." He will rejoin the others when they grow bigger.)

After a while, our kids said their goodbyes to Jerry and the farm owner said we could come and visit him anytime. We drove off, contented in knowing that Jerry had a nice new home.

Which reminds me of an old television show, but not *Seinfeld*. Like the *Jeffersons*, Jerry is definitely "moving on up."

PEPPER, WE HARDLY KNEW YE

Pepper entered our family's life one cold March Saturday morning when I went with a couple of kids to Soulard Market to buy chicken. Not *chicken* like "chicken breast" or "drumsticks" but like, well, Chicken Little. Pepper left us last weekend to go to a "better place" — and that's not just a euphemism.

Our family raises chickens in the back of our Central West End home. For three years we've raised hens to lay eggs and to be pets for our kids.

We lost a couple of hens in the spring — one to natural causes, we think, the other to a menacing raccoon. So, to fill the void, we went to Soulard to buy several $2 chicks.

That morning, we stood in front of the vendor's stall which had a box of chicks covered with a board to keep out the cold wind. Waiting on us was a girl, 11 or 12 years old, and her little brother, who was about six.

The girl took the board off the box and my kids peered in. Running around were various chicks. Some were yellow or white as you'd expect, but some had distinct coloring, including a particularly striking one with black and white feathers.

My kids picked a white one, two red ones… and the speckled one.

As the girl reached for the black-and-white chick, the little boy started protesting. "Sis, you can't give them that one! Daddy said don't sell any of the fancy chicks!"

The girl smiled condescendingly to her little brother and said, "we give the customers what they want." But the boy wouldn't give up. "Daddy will be right back. You'll see!" Meanwhile, we put the chick in our little box and paid the girl. As we walked away, I could still hear the boy protesting.

If you haven't guessed, the "fancy one" was Pepper, named for his salt and pepper feathers. But at the time, we didn't know Pepper was a "he," which led to his ultimate departure.

Vendors normally only sell hen chicks, but they tell you not to be surprised if you end up with a rooster. And if you're raising hens, you don't want a rooster. Why? First, there's a long-standing city ordinance prohibiting roosters. It was written when the city was filled with new residents from the country seeking factory jobs. Second, as roosters mature, their incessant crowing gets louder and more annoying (and we all have neighbors). And as we already learned, roosters become aggressive with hens — trouble in the henhouse.

We'd been through this before; we'd sent a rooster named Jerry a couple of years ago to a friend's farm in House Springs.

It was in June when my wife and kids began to suspect that Pepper — whom I nicknamed "Rod Stewart" because of his spiky feathers — might not share the same gender as the hens. Then one morning, we heard the unmistakable bleat of a young rooster. Pepper's time was nigh.

Our kids and my wife, though, were hoping we might be able to keep Pepper. "He's not that loud," they'd say, or "He's smaller than the girls" (and therefore lower on the pecking order). But you can't mess with nature. Despite what happens in some romantic comedies, men *don't* change.

One morning, when my wife was with our two-year-old in the backyard, Pepper charged them. He was answering some ancient instinct to protect his territory and even though he didn't actually attack, the signs were clear.

What to do? Our friend in House Springs didn't need another rooster.

But then our son, who's studying environmental science and agriculture at Truman State, said he knew a friend who kept chickens and wanted a rooster.

So last weekend, we packed up Pepper in a laundry basket with a cardboard box duct-taped to the top and drove to meet my son for the "chicken exchange."

I've driven many times back and forth to Columbia, but never with a chicken. In fact, I'm sure I'm one of the few people who have ever transported a rooster in a passenger vehicle on I-70.

To his credit, Pepper behaved well on the journey, crowing infrequently from the back of the car. Granted, I had the music turned up, but he was remarkably cooperative.

We met our son and his girlfriend at a park and had a "last supper" with Pepper. Actually, Pepper stayed in his box as we ate our picnic and a steady stream of kids came by to see what was making the noise. My son and his girlfriend drove off with Pepper an hour later.

Tonight I got an email from my son with pictures of Pepper in his new home near Kirksville. Pepper certainly seems happy… his new owners have a couple of acres of land and he has his own coop.

So we couldn't keep the "fancy" chicken after all. I'll have to let that kid at Soulard Market know.

SECTION IV

It's Raining Inside (This *Really* Old House)

CONTROLLING CRITTERS

So, what's a mild-mannered mom to do when she opens a coat closet door and a squirrel scampers by? Or her young children start shrieking in fear because a bushy-tailed intruder is on the kitchen table? Or she opens a desk drawer and "Rocky" pops out?

It's time to take action.

"I love animals and I used to not mind squirrels," said Jane (not her real name). "But when they cross the threshold of my home and endanger my children, that's another story." Thus began Jane's odyssey with what many of us who live in big old homes encounter each fall (drum roll, please): the return of the squirrels.

Jane and her family moved into her home last spring. It's in a neighborhood where big trees and century-old homes make a fine breeding ground for squirrelly interlopers.

I certainly know. When we moved into our house nine years ago, we found out with the first chill of autumn that several other four-legged families also called it home. We would awaken in our bedroom to the sound of squirrels running across the ceiling above us.

After trying many methods, we finally got rid of them using a sonic device that emitted squirrel-unfriendly sounds. But when our boys moved into the third floor, we couldn't use the device. So, we resorted to trapping them and giving them to a friend who is practiced in squirrel removal. Luckily, unlike Jane, we never actually had one running around inside the house.

Jane's troubles started about a month ago. Jane is a friend and I happened to call her one afternoon. In the middle of the conversation, she started screaming. She'd opened a closet and a squirrel had run out.

She grabbed her baby from the floor and when she calmed down, I told her to call a local pest control firm. They came and set some traps in the house.

Two days later, at dinner, Jane heard her six-year-old daughter yelling in the kitchen. Jane ran in to see a squirrel on the table brush by her daughter and run off. The indoor traps hadn't worked.

Later that night, after her husband had assured her he'd gotten the offender out of the house, Jane sat down at her desk in the kitchen. She opened a drawer and up popped a bushy tail.

That was it.

"I resolved to get rid of them, whatever it took," Jane said.

That weekend, her husband was out of town, so my wife and I drove over to Jane's to help her set her own traps on the outside of the house. A few days later she called excitedly: "I caught one! Now what?"

Here comes the part of the story which may offend some. But, if you're Jane and you feel your children are at risk, the well-being of the squirrels isn't your top concern.

Someone suggested a pellet gun. Bad advice.

"I actually drove to Wal-Mart and they're showing me this pellet gun that looks like a real rifle,"she said. "I think, 'I'm an urban liberal who believes in gun control. I can't actually shoot a living thing with that.'

"I also couldn't believe how many guns they sell, but that's another story."

Someone then suggested what Jane calls the "water solution." I won't go into details, but Jane took matters into her own hands. Several squirrels later, all is peaceful at her house.

Some might say she should have trapped the squirrels, and driven ten miles away to a park and released them. But Jane is home all day with three children, including a baby, and it wasn't practical. Besides, she was concerned she might get hurt when she released them.

Understand this: Jane takes no pleasure in the squirrel-removal process. She wishes they'd just go away, or listen to reason. I did tell her that eventually the squirrels will forget that their home was *their* home, but it might take a few years.

And hopefully not another trip to Wal-Mart.

DUMPSTER DREAMS

I got a dumpster.

Parked in front of my house for the past few weeks has been a large rented orange dumpster. It has been slowly filling with construction debris.

For me, that's a status symbol. For years, up and down my street, dumpsters have come and gone as neighbors have added rooms, kitchens, bathrooms or rehabbed the whole house.

While there's been much work on my house, built in 1897, since we bought it in 1992, a lot of it has been done by myself, and not especially well. And I've never needed a dumpster.

Our latest rehab adventure started as so many do: with a crumbling wall and the faint smell of water-soaked plaster.

The bathroom my seven kids use was finally falling apart, from too many showers and too many bad patching jobs I'd done. My first thought was to repair the tile wall again. But that wouldn't fix the water pressure, which had slowed to a dribble.

Realizing I had umpteen years and countless kid showers still ahead, I did something radical: I called a *real* plumber. For years, armed with only a St. Louis Community College "home plumbing" course, I'd done plumbing on a trial (and mostly error) basis. My crowning achievement – or downfall – was a six-month project to put a new bathroom into our third floor. The six months turned into 18 months, complete with several unplanned indoor waterfalls.

But with this latest leak, I thought about something I'd heard on a recent episode of *Prairie Home Companion*, hosted by Garrison Keillor on National Public Radio.

On this show, Keillor talked about the "rugged individualist" Norweigan farmers of northern Minnesota and how they dealt with home improvement projects. "If something broke, no matter what it was, they just figured out how to fix it. This was unlike the yuppies in Minneapolis who believed that there were specialists for everything and it was worth the money to pay someone to do something they did all day."

Bingo. It dawned on me. There are guys who do plumbing all the time, and they're good at it. It was worth the money to pay them to do it right.

Two other things changed my mind: our home equity loan. And my advancing age. Somehow, in my 20s and 30s, I had all kinds of spare time and energy to tackle home projects. I'd stripped old wallpaper from every square inch of the house. I'd painted the outside of the house several times, stood on 30-foot ladders to clean the gutters and crawled through the attic to install insulation. I'd torn out walls and rebuilt with drywall.

And when I did hire contractors, I'd gotten guys on the cheap who were moonlighting for cash. They didn't know anything about permits, rarely showed up on time (or at all) and often looked suspiciously like the FBI posters in the post office.

But now? I finally decided it was time to turn it over to professionals. It was time to think long-term — I didn't want to have to keep patching the bathroom every couple of years into my old age.

At first, Jim Linek from Linek Plumbing said they could do a patch job to improve the water pressure, but as we looked deeper into the problem, it became clear that wouldn't do. Basically, old steel galvanized plumbing had been connected to copper tubing, resulting in a slow clogging of the pipes which would eventually close up and burst. Of course, this steel tubing was buried in the concrete floor of the bathroom and there was no easy way to get to it.

So I sucked it up and agreed to have the bathroom completely gutted, removing all the old plaster walls and concrete floor, and start over.

Linek would be the plumber and general contractor.

As we talked, I negotiated a way that I could still be a part of the process. I told Linek I could do the "demo" work and the painting.

If you haven't done it, demolition work is, well, a lot of fun. For a week, my son James and I took a hammer and crowbar and ripped out the thick old plaster walls and ceiling. There is a certain thrill to taking a sledgehammer and (wearing OSHA-approved goggles and dust masks) smashing into a decrepit old toilet that always made funny noises. Then we tossed the debris out the window and it went down a wooden chute.

Once we had our fun, the professionals took over. Day after day at 7 a.m., some contractor would cheerfully arrive to do their plumbing, electric or carpentry work. I was amazed at how quickly, cleanly and efficiently they worked. One day, the plumber explained to me what a terrible job the previous plumber had done on the third-floor bathroom. I nodded knowingly; "Yeah, we've had some real losers work here."

At the beginning of the project, there were several days when all nine people in our house shared a single bathroom — ours. Later, we all used the same shower, including a span over the holidays when six more relatives stayed here. Family togetherness? You bet.

The work is winding down. There are a few finishing items, but the bathroom is nearly ready to accept the teenage shower onslaught. We've done the painting and now we realize the new kids' bathroom is the nicest room in the house. But that's OK; soon, my wife and I will have ours back again, and we'll no longer be subject to day-and-night interlopers.

Outside, the dumpster is filled to the top and they're coming to take it away in a few days. I think I'm going to miss it.

LIVING ON THE PRIVATE PLACES

Years ago, the editor of the *West End Word* came into my office to let me know about a call she'd just gotten. It was from a neighborhood reader who'd complained about an article we'd done. "It was a private place resident," she sighed. "You know how they are."

At the time, I was living in a small three-bedroom house in University City with four kids and one bathroom. My editor's implication was that "private place" people were snooty and elitist.

Little did I know that in a couple of years I'd become one of them.

The Central West End boasts a number of historic private streets, from the grand mansions on Westmoreland and Portland Places to more modest streets like mine. The concept has its origins in Julius Pitzman, a surveyor and urban designer in the late 1800s who laid out most of the city's private places.

Then, as now, Pitzman's idea was to create little communities of homes that were separated to some degree from the surrounding neighborhood. In the 1800s, this was done to give wealthy industrialists an island of custom homes cut off from the smoke, grime and high density of urban life.

But what Pitzman didn't know at the time was that 70 years after many of these homes were built, the private streets weren't elitist… they helped to save the neighborhood.

In the 1960s, so-called "white flight" caused many longtime city residents to flee to the suburbs. Ten years later, urban pioneers started to buy up the big old homes and renovate them.

Not everyone left, though, and some who stayed and grew old in their homes also developed a jaundiced view of the changing neighborhood. (It was probably one of these people that my editor spoke with.)

In the 1970s and 1980s, in addition to the original private streets with big mansions and elaborate gates, other city streets petitioned to have their street closed. The theory was that if a street was blocked off, it would impede traffic and "drive through" riff-raff.

This is was what happened to my street. It wasn't originally designed as private; indeed, it originally had a bus line and busy traffic from nearby Kingshighway and Union Boulevards.

But as neighborhoods started changing for the worse in the 1960s, there was a rush to block off streets. Now there are so many that you need a map to navigate from one end to another. I remember one night, not long after we moved into our house, a fire truck screamed down our street. I watched it out the window and saw it drive to the end of our block and then have to turn around and race back when it couldn't go through.

When I tell people now where I live, some say, "Oh you live in those big houses." I race to explain that no, we're not in the big mansions, that we bought our house in the early 1990s for less than $150,000 and we have a lot of kids and need a big house. It's as if I'm trying to convince them that I'm not one of those snooty private place people.

All of this came to mind recently when a rapid series of e-mails bounced around the residents on our street. The subject? Installing more gates on the street to thwart parking interlopers and petty criminals. The new gates would also block pedestrians from easy access on the sidewalks.

One of my neighbors at one end of the street has had a series of break-ins and expensive artwork stolen. On the other end, another neighbor has had their portable basketball hoop knocked over four times and is now broken. Others complain about non-residents parking in front of their homes.

I can't necessarily blame them for wanting more security, but are more gates the answer?

The fact is, most of us live here because we like the city and its diversity. If we wanted to get away from people, we'd move to Wildwood and their three-acre lots and "gated communities."

Blocking off streets and sidewalks and putting up gates illustrates the tension we feel as city dwellers: we like the city atmosphere, yet we want to block off our homes to restrict access from the "wrong people." How much of the city do we want to let in — or keep out? More gates would simply impede the parade of joggers, pedestrians, bus riders, students and others who give the city its character.

After all, you know how *they* are.

HAPPY ANNIVERSARY, HOUSE

The other morning, my wife said, "Happy anniversary," and smiled.

What? Anniversary? Panic raced through me. Did I forget…

"Thirteen years ago today we moved into this house," she said.

"Oh, great," I said, trying not show my immense relief. "That's nice."

Later, I started thinking about it. In 1992, we moved our family with four kids from a small one bathroom bungalow in University City to our home on Westminster Place in the Central West End.

It was our fifth move in seven years of marriage, which had included California and Colorado. I had been looking for a bigger house since we'd moved to University City, and had fallen in love with the big old houses on the tree-lined streets of the "central corridor." We found a home on Westminster Place, but the deal fell apart literally on the day of closing, my wife eight and a half months pregnant, and the movers ready to pack up.

That was hugely disappointing, but fate eventually intervened. I heard about another house on the block, but I didn't tell my wife and I went to look at it. It was much larger, and with my 32-year-old eyes, the rusting-steel-sink kitchen, cigarette-smoke stained wallpaper, green shag carpet and 14 weed trees in the backyard didn't deter me. It had a turret with curved-glass windows, a spacious front hall, four big bedrooms on the second floor and a third floor with a lot of potential and it sat on a large lot. One of the best omens when I toured the house was that as I walked from room to room, the owner had radios tuned to the baseball game. That's my kind of house!

I finally told my wife, the owners took our first offer ($142,000 I'm not ashamed to say), and we began moving in. By then our fourth child had been born.

Sometimes I wonder what happened to my 30's; that period is such a blur. When I think about it, I realize I did only two things: work on the house and help raise babies. It began with making 64 trips (I counted) with our mini-van filled with boxes from our house in University City to our new house. Movers moved the big stuff, but I stacked the boxes in our big front hall. Little by little, the boxes were emptied and it was at least three months before they were gone.

What followed was 10 years of mostly trial and error with home improvement. Our overriding philosophy was, "Do it right," if we had the money or not. I sometimes wonder what the "worst job" was. Was it crawling through the third floor walls, sweaty and sticky in 95-degree heat, trying to stuff fiberglass insulation between the floor joists? Or climbing a 30-foot aluminum ladder next to a power line in the middle of winter to chip away an ice dam in our gutter? I do know what was the most fun: deciding "what the hell" at midnight and swinging my crowbar into a bad 30-year-old drywall bathroom to reveal the original high ceilings and woodwork. Nothing like a little demolition for stress-relief and therapy.

Along the way we discovered the history of the house and a wonderful neighborhood — we even heard that singer Liza Minelli and broadcaster Bob Costas visited here (on separate occasions). Despite disbelief from our county friends and family, it's been a great place to raise kids. But make no mistake: we moved in when the area was well on its way to rejuvenation. The real "urban pioneers" were in the 1970s and 1980s when big houses like mine could be bought for $20,000 and many were vacant. I remember when my wife's cousin first came to visit our street, he looked around and said, "This isn't the city." He was right; it's always been our little Shangri-La.

Now I'm in my mid-40s, and my opinion of home improvement has changed. We've pretty much been through the entire house and yard once. It's been painted, air-conditioned, plumbed, and we have a new kids' bathroom and a 10-year-old rehabbed kitchen we can live with. I no longer get on the ladder anymore, to chip ice or paint. In fact it takes a lot for me to do a project now. When bricks started falling out of the wall recently near our front door, I finally got off the couch. I'm more likely to write a check (even if we still can't afford it) these days than to pick up a tool. Over the years I've found a reliable group of handymen and contractors who can do the job a lot more quickly and better than I can. And — believe it or not young parents – children actually grow up to be helpful.

One of the best things about the neighborhood was that even though I had grown up in the county, when we moved to the CWE it was like discovering a whole new city. Sure, I'd gone to Forest Park as a kid, but I had no idea about the richness of the culture, architecture, history and diversity.

In the years we've lived here, a lot has happened around us. The Chase Park Plaza reopened, St. Louis and Washington University transformed, Barnes Hospital expanded into its own small city, Grand Center bloomed, Forest Park was renovated and there has been a building boom of new and rehabbed housing throughout the neighborhood. Block-by-block, from the new homes in Gaslight Square to the high-rises on Skinker Boulevard, people are discovering what we found 13 years ago.

One of my theories is that it starts with the housing stock. The elegant brick homes and buildings built here beginning more than 100 years ago may have had their ups and downs, but well-built neighborhoods will eventually keep their value and appreciate. This is certainly true on our street. I could hardly afford to move in here now.

Of course there are problems... "challenges"... to our wonderful central corridor lifestyle. The flip side of highly valuable real estate means fewer housing opportunities for young families and working people. Although we have a wonderful network of private and parochial schools, the city's public schools continue to struggle with deep-seated problems. MetroLink was a great idea, but the "cross-county extension" envisioned to link the CWE with Clayton and south county has become bogged down in cost overruns and tear-your-hair-out traffic congestion. Under the leadership of Police Chief Joe Mokwa, major crime in the area has dropped to near-record lows for the area, but petty crimes like panhandling, license-tag removal and car break-ins still nag the area.

But the future looks bright. Once MetroLink is finally done, a lawyer in Clayton can walk a few blocks to take a train downtown to court or whisk home to Shrewsbury without battling traffic. A medical student at Washington University can either go downtown for a night out on Laclede's Landing, or home to his apartment in University City. Even a family in St. Charles can park at the North Hanley station to go to the Zoo, a baseball game or to the Taste of Clayton in Shaw Park.

For myself, I joke that the next move from our house will be in a "pine box." We've met wonderful neighbors who are in their 70s and 80s who have lived in the neighborhood 50 or 60 years. I still envision a day 30 years from now when I will be out front of my house, slowly sweeping the sidewalk, and one of my kids will drive by, and yell out of the window, "Dad, when are you going to move out of that big old house?"

THE WINDOW UNITS WILL KILL ME

The one home-improvement job I always figured would kill me was the twice-annual ritual of installing and removing window air conditioners in our house, built in 1897.

It's more dangerous than chipping ice dams out of the third story gutters, retrieving traps filled with snarling, rabid squirrels, or installing rolls of fiberglass insulation in our 200-degree attic in the summer.

Why? As my age increases, and gravity strengthens, the task of lugging eight window units to three levels of my house has become increasingly hazardous. And since most of the units are 400-pound hand-me-downs from the last century, the prospect of losing my footing in the back staircase seems more and more likely. One year, when I had to remove a unit that didn't work, I simply pushed it out a second story window, being careful that no flower beds or cherished pets were in the way.

But now, thanks to a historically low refinance rate on my house's mortgage, my wife and my insurance agent can cross "home improvement hazard #1" off my list.

We're getting central air.

That may not be a big deal to most, but my wife and I realized recently that neither of us have ever lived in a building with central air conditioning... that's a total of 84 years.

We both grew up in St. Louis in old houses in "inner ring" suburbs — Clayton and Richmond Heights. My parents eventually got central air in their "big old house," but only after I moved out.

But even when we moved out of town, we either lived in old homes and apartments or in climates that didn't require air conditioning. We lived in Westminster, California, near Los Angeles, in an apartment close enough to the beach that we didn't need it. Later we moved to Highlands Ranch, Colorado, near Denver, at an altitude of 6,000 feet, and even though it was a brand new house, no one needed central air there, either.

When we moved back to St. Louis in 1989, we first lived in a small, old house in University City. Eleven years ago, we moved into our current house in the Central West End. Through all of these years of home ownership, I collected used window units from family and neighbors. I could have left the air conditioners in the windows permanently, but I used to be a house painter and I know what water damage can do to old double-hung wood windows.

Of course, this isn't just about "my needs." The other driving factor for central air was the upper respiratory tracts of several of my children, including two with asthma. After last spring's season of sneezing, coughing and illness, I knew it was time.

When I was a kid, only my parents had a window unit in their bedroom. I remember trying anything I could to stay up in their room, but eventually we'd be sent to bed. On really hot nights, when I slept on the top bunk, I'd take a shower and not dry off, turning the window fan on "high." I remember my Dad once reasoning that kids, being smaller, could tolerate the heat better.

My kids would never accept that reasoning — yes it is a different world — and they would tire of hearing my "I-walked-three-miles-to-school" stories about the deprivation I suffered without central air.

But maybe, when one of them gets old enough, I can make them deal with the snarling, rabid squirrels.

I FOUGHT THE LAWN

I walked out of the house last week and saw my across-the-street neighbor performing his weekly manicure of his "perfect" front lawn.

He's very meticulous; he cuts it with an electric mower, trims and rakes.

I've long given up trying — or caring — to keep up with him and other neighbors with perfect lawns.

As I've written about before, I have a "city lawn," a loose collection of green plants — some of them actually grass — that cover my land. As long as it's cut, hey, it's all green.

But I'm a man, and proud, and the sight of my neighbor made me realize it had been a while since I'd cut the grass.

One reason is that our front yard is small, shaded and not watered very often, so it really doesn't grow quickly. My back yard is another story, but it's out of sight, at least from the neighbors.

So I've adopted what's called a "mullet" lawn. A mullet is a bad hair style from the 1970s that featured short hair in front and long in back. It even had a motto.... "Business in front, party in back." That's my lawn.

Another reason is I'm using a new kind of lawn mower this year. It's an old-fashioned "push mower," the kind that relies not on fossil fuel but, well, my fuel.

I'd like to say I got it to save gasoline, reduce pollution and get more exercise. But the fact is that when I went out to the garage last spring to get my mower, it had been stolen.

What to do? I've been very hard on power lawn mowers over the years. For many summers, I would buy a used lawn mower for $25 to $50, run it into the ground, and leave it in the alley when it died.

When I bought a new mower, I'd get the $99 special at Home Depot (always assembled) and also run it into the ground. I knew I was supposed to check and change the oil, clean the air filter, etc., but it was just too much trouble. I'd just leave it in the garage in the winter and hope it would start up in the spring.

This past spring, when I realized I had no mower, I went to Home Depot, saw the $99 special and.... I just couldn't do it. I was tired of the noise, the smoke and the rocks, broken sticks and plastic toys spitting out the side. I was tired of running to the gas station with $1.50 in my pocket to fill the gas can and it spilling on the back seat.

There was also the fear in the back of my mind of the blade flying off the bottom of the mower and spinning across the yard. I'm sure that fear is from an "urban legend" I heard as a wide-eyed kid. A boy had his head cut off by a spinning blade as his dad cut the lawn.

So at Home Depot I decided to try the push mower. Even though I have a fear about *those*. I still have a scar from when I was a kid playing with my Dad's push mower —trying to break a stick in the blades — and it sliced my hand. Pick your childhood fear to conquer, I guess.

When I got the mower home, I realized it wasn't assembled. So I did what any man would do: I told my mechanically-inclined son to put it together.

When I started to cut the lawn, I enjoyed the quiet "swish" of the blades, the lack of smoke and projectiles, and even the physical exertion. There was no gas to fill, no oil to spray and less chance of accidentally mowing down my wife's flowers.

But what I realized quickly was that my new mower didn't exactly cut *everything* in its path. While it did fine with real grass, it didn't cut as well the wealth of crabgrass and weeds in my yard. If I had a "perfect" lawn, it would do fine.

Still, when I finished, if I stood back far enough, it seemed like it had been cut. Sure, it wasn't the razor-sharp cut of a violent power-mower, but it was, well, good enough. About what a "city lawn" deserves.

IT'S RAINING INSIDE

"Daddy it's raining inside."

My seven-year-old son told me that one recent Friday night. I was in the third floor of our 100-plus-year-old house, finishing setting wall tile in the bathroom I'd been working on for more than a year. Oh no, I thought: another water emergency.

In a flash (or a flush?), the entire project passed before my eyes. I'd started full of hope in early 1998, determined to restore a bathroom that hadn't been used for 30 years. With the oldest of my five sons turning 13 and planning to move to the third floor, I knew I'd need it for years to come.

In some ways, it was the ideal place to "experiment." No one lived up there so I could take my time and not worry about tearing up the room. I'd done plenty of painting and drywall work before and the electrical work had already been done, so the plumbing was the biggest challenge. I'd fixed leaky faucets, installed a sink and taken a course at St. Louis Community College. Best of all, my wife's uncle was a retired plumber who could help out in a jam.

What I thought was a three-month project turned into much more.

The biggest problem was installing new water lines from the third floor to the basement. This meant tearing a wall out in my son Danny's room. Luckily, he's patient; he spent much of last summer sleeping elsewhere. Some nights, he go door to door, asking if he could sleep in a sibling's room, hoping for a vacancy.

Before this water emergency, one other had occurred, also on a Friday night. That was the first time I turned the water on in the new pipes. Remember the phrase, "a thousand points of light"? I experienced "a thousand pin holes of water" as tiny leaks sprouted from the pipe joints. I spent the rest of the weekend fixing those. I was then able to restore my son's wall — and him to his bed — in time for school last fall.

Months went by with little or no work done, especially around the holidays. But with summer coming, I hoped to finish before it got too hot.

The last major plumbing work was to hook up the drain pipes from the toilet, sink and bathtub. I tested it carefully — I poured gallons of water from a milk jug down each drain to make sure the main "stack" was clear. The water flowed.

But on that recent Friday night, it flowed elsewhere. I ran downstairs to find my wife calmly embroidering on the family room couch as water poured through a doorway. She'd seen this before. I spent the rest of the evening looking in vain for a leak.

My wife's uncle the plumber came over the next morning and we finally found the problem — guess where — in the wall of my son

Danny's room. It turned out that the "stack," unused for 30 years, had accumulated rust and had stopped up. So I tore out the wall and had the roto-rooter guy clean it out, and Danny was out of his room again.

I'm now in the final stages of painting. It won't be long before I turn the bathroom over to teenagers and guests. It will be the last big plumbing project I undertake. Danny won't let me go near his wall again.

BUT DOES IT SMELL?

One man's trash…

A couple of Saturdays ago, I was with my son James. We were driving our 1998 eight-seat Dodge van (also known as the "church bus" because of all the kids we haul around) very slowly down the pothole-happy alley behind our house.

As we drove, out of the corner of my eye I noticed a chair sitting next to a dumpster. My son, who along with my wife is a veteran dumpster diver, immediately pointed it out.

Normally, I would mutter something about having too much stuff in the house already, but for some reason I took a closer look.

There sat what appeared to be a perfectly nice wicker easy chair. It looked like it came right off the showroom floor at Pier 1 Imports.

I don't have anything in principle against dumpster diving, but I've always felt my role in the family is the Guy Who Gets Rid Of Stuff. I take out all the trash and I see the alley as a place to dispose of things, not as an open-air flea market.

But when I saw that chair, I realized: hey, we could *use* a wicker easy chair. I looked closer at the wicker chair. I was sure there was a missing leg or a gash in the back. But I lifted it up, turned it around, and was amazed to find it intact. In that instant, my world view changed. I had joined the legion of otherwise normal people who prowl city alleys for "you-haul-it-you-have-it" items.

The chair wasn't the first thing I'd rescued from the alley. I had snared a decorative plaster-of-paris bird bath and for some reason, a couple of old odd-sized wooden doors. But these things remained *outside*. The mark of a true diver is one who risks bringing things in the house.

My wife has been at it for years. I'm not surprised anymore to come home to find various things on our front porch. They sit there "airing out" before the final transition of moving inside. A sort-of "get acquainted" period.

Among her finds? A cushioned chair acquired from a dumpster at a seminary. Two free-standing brass lamps that needed rewiring. A perfectly fine wooden dresser that she later painted in a *SpongeBob* motif for a church auction. A set of wooden steps she also painted as a flower-pot holder.

A friend of ours had a husband who was a dedicated diver. They had a small city house, and our friend barely tolerated his acquisitions. She finally came up with two rules about his alley treasures: they couldn't smell and they couldn't block her path to the washing machine.

Her husband also had the annoying habit when she was driving to suddenly yell "Slow down," so he could hop out and inspect a possible find.

I doubt I'll get that bad, but you never know. After we picked up the wicker chair, I found another chair before we left the alley. It smelled a little, but I'll just leave it on the front porch for a while.

LIGHTS OUT ACROSS ST. LOUIS (2008)

Has it really been a year since the "lights went out in St. Louis"?

It's certainly a year that Ameren UE won't soon forget. The company has faced two major power outages, and in December 2005, the Taum Sauk dam burst.

I thought about all this recently when the power in our house flickered momentarily.

I had a flashback to July 2007 and suddenly everything I did with electricity was on my mind. From the electric shaver to the air conditioning, to the computer and television to my alarm clock flashing "12:00."

So where were you when the power died?

Me? I'll never forget because I was in a basement in Kirkwood with five other middle-aged guys, playing guitar. I'm in a band of old high school buddies and we were having "practice" — OK, having fun.

It was about 7 p.m. on July 19. The power flickered and then went out. We were in the middle of a song and we kept playing, not knowing exactly what was going on. We actually finished the song; but like everyone else in St. Louis, we didn't think it would be dark for long. The song we were playing (no kidding)? *Stormy*.

My first thought when it happened, after all of the extreme heat that month, was maybe it was caused by a "brown out." Remember those? Growing up in the 60s and 70s, there would be occasional power shortages during hot weather and our groaning old window air conditioning units would hiss and die. At night, my brothers and sisters and I would take cold showers and use window fans. But we were kids then.

When the power went out last year, being in a basement with small windows, we had no idea what was going on. But when my friend's wife and kids came down the stairs talking about tornado warnings, we knew something was up.

As we stood around in the dark, I smugly told the other guys, all of whom live in St. Louis county, "Oh, we never lose power in the city." Other than a few flickers, we'd never lost power in 14 years of living in the Central West End. But driving home that night from Kirkwood, the only lights I saw on were headlights. Trees were down everywhere, even blocking a couple of streets near my house. It seemed I'd landed on a different planet.

When I got home, one of my sons and his girlfriend were eating dinner by candlelight as if nothing had happened. "Hi Dad, how's it going?" Being the "eco kid" in our family, I think he was actually enjoying it. Until, of course, he needed to recharge his iPod.

We were lucky in many ways. First, my wife and most of my kids happened to be out of town, so they were spared. Second, power at my office was on, so I didn't have to worry about fried computers or lost data. And after one warm night in our house, by 2 p.m. the next day our power was back.

That night we had a "power party" for our neighbors, grilling all kinds of food that they pulled from their lifeless freezers. It was a lot of fun, but became less fun for my neighbors on the other side of the street as their power stayed off for a week.

When power was finally restored to the hundreds of thousands of people in the area, like others, I began to make a mental checklist of things I'd learned and should do to be prepared for the next time.

I used to make fun of my oldest son's survivalist tendencies. But right after the outage I found myself stumbling around my house looking for working flashlights and candles. I started to wonder exactly what my son had stored in the corner of our basement. I found a few old cans of beans and a Pine Valley water jug. I looked at the green slime in the jug and wondered: is algae a bad thing? We clearly wouldn't survive long.

Afterwards, I remember getting into a long conversation with an engineering-minded neighbor about portable generators. He was going to wait a while to let prices go down, but had already researched various models and how much power they could provide. He'd also determined where and how he'd store the gasoline to run them, because gasoline pumps might not work.

At the time all of that seemed like the sensible thing to do. And then last December another big storm caused area-wide outages, though we were spared. It was another reminder that I really need to be better prepared.

So how ready am I now, a year after the blackout?

I wonder if a *lot* of algae is a bad thing.

WATER, WATER EVERYWHERE

There's a new movie out, ***Master and Commander,*** with Russell Crowe playing the part of a brave sea captain. I haven't seen the movie, but that's OK. It can serve as a bad analogy for my hero fantasy when dealing with a plumbing crisis at my house last week. Here are the entries from my ship's log:

Tuesday.

4 p.m. The furnace guy is at our house trying to get our 50-year-old boiler working. My wife calls and says, "You'd better come home." The problem? The furnace guy was replacing the water supply valve and a gush of water shot forth. Turns out the water line comes directly from the street and there is no shut-off valve. Furnace guy says, "I can't help you. I'm not a plumber." We're taking on water. The captain must act.

5 p.m. I call the city water department to shut off the water at the street. "Sorry, we can't get anyone there until tomorrow," he said. "You'll have to call a plumber." I try to protest and hang up on the guy in frustration. The captain is starting to lose it.

6 p.m. I call five plumbers. The only one I reach says, "I might be able to shut it off, but that's really the water department's problem. It'll cost $250 for me to try." I have this theory about some contractors: they have a meter on their phone that registers how desperate your voice sounds when you call, with a corresponding charge. I sound desperate, but no way I'm paying that much. So much for calm in the face of a storm.

6:30 p.m. My helpful neighbor, having already driven to several hardware stores looking to buy a special doo-dad "key" (official name unknown) to shut off the water, arrives back empty-handed. "They won't sell me one," he said. "You have to be a licensed plumber." Suddenly, he flags down another neighbor, who works for the fire department. We explain the problem and he races off to his fire station to retrieve a doo-dad key. Great I think, we captains stick together.

7 p.m. Despite a half-hour of work, we still can't shut it off. It appears the valve is broken. I thank both neighbors and they go home to their safely-pressurized water systems. My gusher is still gushing. The ship is starting to list.

8 p.m. I call the water department again. This time I'm calm and

rational. I apologize for hanging up earlier. The guy laughs and says don't worry about it. Then, before I have the chance to plead, beg and offer up one of my children, he tells me he'll send a crew over that evening. Help is on its way!

Meanwhile, my wife and children have abandoned ship. They've gone off to my parents' house where the three teenagers will have hot showers and toilets that flush. The captain is not leaving the ship, come hell or…. wait, I have high water.

9 p.m. Water department crew number one arrives. By this time, our balmy weather day has turned to cold and drizzle. No matter to me. I'm standing out there until they're done. A captain sticks with his crew. Coffee, anyone? I'm buying…

9:30 p.m. Crew number one gives up. "We'll call the digging crew." Don't leave, mateys! I plead. They assure me another crew will arrive.

10:30 p.m. Crew number two arrives. Two pleasant guys get out and have the same trouble shutting it off. "Guess we'll have to dig it out," one says. "With a backhoe?" I ask. "No, we use shovels." Wow, I'm impressed. I offer coffee and mentally compose a new version of the Budweiser radio commercial, "Real Men of Genius," featuring the Water-Valve-Digger-Up-Guys.

11 p.m. I keep running in and out of the house to check the geyser as the water guys struggle to shut it off. First, it slows to a mild torrent, and eventually to a slow trickle. Finally, it stops. We've plugged the leak! I thank the guys and send them off to their next emergency. I'm too tired to do anything but fall into bed. The captain stays with the ship, even with no water or heat.

Wednesday

9 a.m. I call a plumber who has done a lot of work on my house a few years back. "I'll have him come by around noon," the pleasant-sounding receptionist says. I go to work and await his call.

2 p.m. No call yet. "Oh, he's finishing up at the work site. He should be calling you any minute."

5 p.m. No call from the plumber and no answer from the pleasant-sounding receptionist. I'm not feeling too pleasant.

6 p.m. Forget the ship. The captain is tired and needs a hot shower and a shot of rum. I bail out and join my family at my parents' house. The ship could sink for all I care.

Thursday

9 a.m. A plumber says he's on his way. No, I mean he's *really* on his way. A few hours later, a nice young man from Linek Plumbing Company arrives. I offer coffee.

12 p.m. The plumber finishes. We have water! I call the furnace guy to get the boiler fixed and running.

4 p.m. The water is on, the furnace is running, Old Faithful has stopped and the captain and his family are tired, but warm and hydrated. The ship has righted and steams on.

Hero or not, I could do without a sequel.

Scarlet

CHICKEN JOURNAL:

CHICKENS ARE PUNNY

I was feeling a little **cooped up.**

It was somewhere around Paducah, Tennessee, and we had just a few hours left on our 850 mile trek home from our family vacation in South Carolina. There were seven of us in a mini-van, including a three-month old baby and four other kids.

It wasn't that the kids were acting up – they're actually good car travelers. Maybe it was endless miles and the drone of the "best loved children's songs" CD that was playing. We'd put it on since the Nashville National Public Radio station had fuzzed out right in the middle of *Prairie Home Companion* (apparently northern Kentucky/southern Illinois is somewhat of a cultural wasteland, but I didn't say that.)

Anyway, one of the kids said they couldn't wait to see our pet chickens back home and I was seized with a thought to alleviate highway boredom. I started thinking about all the sayings that have something to do with chickens. My wife got out a pad and paper and the kids chimed in.

There are a lot of chicken-related sayings. My wife suggested that it had to do with the fact that at one time the city was full of the animals. There was a, well, **chicken in every pot.**

In the 19th and early 20th centuries, new urban dwellers brought their chickens with them from the farm. In fact, they were so plentiful in the streets of St. Louis that the *St. Louis Post-Dispatch* had a popular weekly column called "Chicken Corner" for poultry-raising readers. But eventually, due to modernization or perhaps ambitious health department workers, the city passed an ordinance limiting each household to a maximum of four animals and they became as **rare as hen's teeth**. People started buying eggs and boneless chicken breasts at the grocery store instead of grabbing them from a coop.

Still, chickens remain in our everyday language. And frankly, many of the sayings aren't complimentary. Chickens aren't the brightest eggs in the basket, and the sayings refer to their tendencies to be skittish, scared and scatter-brained. But perhaps the reason so many of these sayings became clichés is that we're a lot closer to our feathered friends on the genetic tree than we think.

One of my favorite is **pecking order.** Before I had kids, I used to think the "birth order" theories were just psychological mumbo-jumbo. But it's true: in families, there are similarities between children based on when they are born. But, lacking beaks, kids tend to exert their authority over lesser siblings with other means of control, like access to video games.

Feeling **hen-pecked?** I better be careful here; some of the sayings have to do with the fact that large groups of female chickens live together. I don't want to get someone **madder than a wet hen.**

But men don't fare much better. Roosters by nature are loud, aggressive, and, well, **cocky.** They always have **something to crow about.**

As far as young children, it'd be great if for once at bedtime they'd **go to sleep with the chickens,** which is right at dusk. But eventually they will grow up and **flee the coop** (at least that's what I've heard). But what **empty nester** still doesn't want his kids to **come home to roost** (just temporarily, of course)?

Some of human nature's less-than-stellar characteristics are ascribed to chickens. A young child's penmanship — or a doctor's prescription-writing – is called **chicken scratch**. This refers I believe to the birds' habit of tearing up with their claws whatever piece of ground they're living on. If you're scared, cowardly or brash, you're called, well, a **chicken.** Or **chicken-hearted,** as I heard a network broadcaster recently call terrorists. A particularly foolish game of teenagers aiming their cars at each other and then turning at the last second is known as **playing chicken.** And on vacation you're in line to take the Death on Wheels roller coaster at the amusement park because your kids talked you into it? Go ahead and **chicken out.**

Do you have teenagers? Their mood swings are often exasperating. One minute, they're a **good egg**, but they will eventually **get your hackles up** (hackles are the feathers around a chicken's neck). Especially if your son is a **chick magnet** and spends all night on the phone.

If you're so busy and harried getting ready for your family vacation that you lose your keys, then you **run around like a chicken with its head cut off** (which, for a chicken, is a lot worse than losing keys). Just calm down, Mr. **Feather Brain.** Let your wife drive and have a **cocktail.**

Back in the car driving home from vacation, we found another NPR station near Carbondale, indicating that we were near civilization again. After a fun week with the kids eating too much and spending our **nest egg**, I looked forward to getting back home and back to routine.

It even occurred to me that our three oldest kids, who had arrived home a day earlier, might have spent the day cleaning up the house, cutting the lawn and making dinner for us when we arrived.

But you know what they say. **Don't count your chickens before they're hatched.**

SECTION V

A Hobby is This Close to Mental Disease

(Dad's Life)

TWO WEDDINGS AND A FUNERAL: SAGA OF THE BLUE BLAZER

I put my "blue blazer" sports coat into the armoire last week and reached into a pocket. I pulled out three pieces of paper: two wedding announcements and a prayer card.

The weddings included a cousin and a business associate. The funeral was for one of my favorite uncles.

In the past month or so, I realized the sports coat had traveled with me to Portland, Oregon; Hendersonville, North Carolina; and north county in St. Louis. I couldn't remember when it had seen so much use.

Twenty years ago, when I started my career, my parents bought me the blazer, some ties and several pairs of khaki pants. Having put me through college, they outfitted me for the working world, a mysterious place where everybody showed up at 8 a.m., drank coffee, and talked at the water cooler (whatever that was).

As I got older, working styles changed and I put away my blazer and ties. I still wore khakis, but the dress shirts and loafers were replaced by golf shirts and comfortable shoes.

I wore the blue blazer less and less; it hung in my closet waiting for the occasional appearance at church or with my banker.

The weddings were joyous events. My cousin Diane was married in Portland, a part of the country I'd never visited. She's the only girl in a family of seven. Her father died when she was young, and her six brothers walked her down the aisle to "give her away."

I spent the weekend with my sisters and my parents, renewing old ties. With a network of cousins in our Irish-German families, I realized I was lucky growing up. Cousins were like siblings without the rivalry. You saw them periodically at family gatherings and you shared a familiarity you didn't have with even your best friends.

I was reminded of this during the wedding weekend when I visited my cousin Mike Fister in Oregon. Mike would qualify as a family success story. He is C.E.O. of a big software company and counts Bill Gates among his business peers. We went to his palatial home near Salem, a four-level mansion cut into the hillside above a lake, with sailboats and a large wine cellar. But when I first saw him, he gave me a goofy grin and squeezed my hand until my fingers almost broke. Good old Mike. Even wearing Italian loafers and a GQ suit, he was the same mischievous older cousin who used to hip-check me into the bushes when playing basketball and dunk me in the pool.

A few weeks later, I traveled to the Smoky Mountains in North Carolina for another reunion with cousins, but on a much sadder note. My Uncle Al Hughes had died, and once again I saw aunts and uncles I hadn't seen in a while. Al was the classic "fun uncle," a great storyteller who loved kids and jazz music. He had an eternally optimistic outlook despite losing a daughter to cancer when she was still a young woman. He survived World War II, daily two-hour-long train commutes from New Jersey to Manhattan, and had retired with my aunt in Hendersonville, N.C.

But retirement was only the beginning of Al's life. An engineer who spent his career at the New York city phone company, he began teaching math as a volunteer at a small parochial school near his home. He also recorded his voluminous collection of old 78 rpm jazz records onto cassette tape and cds, and shared his love of Sidney Bechet and Glen Miller at local community college lectures and radio stations.

At his memorial service, Al's son-in-law Walter Sorrells (an award-winning mystery novelist) described Al as "one of the good guys." Like Tom Brokaw's "greatest generation," my uncle was one of those hard-working, self-effacing, always-smiling people who rode over the bumps in their lives knowing they were going in the right direction.

Later that night, I was with my brother and sister and a bunch of cousins, drinking beer and singing and telling stories late into the night. I thought to myself that as we all aged, it was sad to think that we'd be gathering more in the future for funerals instead of weddings.

I left North Carolina without my blue blazer. I had forgotten it in my hotel room; but luckily my parents were staying another night and they said they'd retrieve it. I told them just to hang onto it, even though they didn't plan to be back in St. Louis for another few weeks.

But my Mom went to the UPS store and sent it back in a few days; "You never know when you'll need it," she said.

Like all mothers, she was right. A week later I went to the wedding of the daughter of Rob Patel, who owns Presto Printing in the Central West End, and I pulled out the trusty sports coat.

But this was no ordinary wedding, at least not for me. Rob is Hindu and the wedding was a traditional Indian affair. The bride, groom and wedding family all wore traditional clothing and the ceremony was performed on an elaborate stage decorated like an Indian palace. The room was filled with dark-skinned men and women dressed in colorful, beautiful saris.

St. Louis being the town that it is, I even I saw people I knew. Karen Duffy, owner of Duff'restaurant, and Carolyn Toft, former executive director of Landmarks Association, were in attendance.

Being a Catholic, I was used to long weddings, but this service was almost two hours long. But it was fascinating, as the celebrant stopped periodically to explain the Hindu ceremony in English. The service included a series of symbolic acts, such as the couple throwing butter and rice into a fire to honor Agni, the goddess of fire, power and purity. At the end of the service, those in attendance were given a handful of flower petals to shower on the new couple.

We ate a tasty curry-based lunch and afterwards I thought how marriages are the beginning of something new; and so are funerals, in a way.

We drove home and I put the blazer in the armoire, where it will await its next call of duty.

CALIFORNIA DREAMIN'

My sister came in town recently for a visit, and she arrived healthier, tanner and happier than I'd seen her in years.

What was her secret? Last fall she moved from St. Louis to California. Since moving there, she's hiked mountains, found a personal trainer, joined an amateur Scottish dancing troupe and engaged in "pranic healing" (whatever that is).

It reminded me of twenty years ago when I packed up my yellow Ford Fiesta and pointed it west. After living in St. Louis my entire life, I moved to California. Go West, Young Man, and all that.

"Going to California " has almost become an American metaphor for change or rebirth (especially if you're from the east or midwest). Anyone who's had enough of ice storms and humid heat waves, and has nothing to lose, can pack up the car and head west to start a new life.

For me, the fascination with California started at a young age and was linked to music. When I was 12 years old, in the middle of winter, I remember going out to the garage where my brother's Pinto was parked. I climbed into the back seat, turned on the battery, and played his 8-track album, *Best of the Beach Boys Vol. 1*.

That was before I had my own albums. My brother played the tape as he drove carpool each morning, and I just couldn't get the music out of my head. The catchy hooks, lush vocals and California imagery was enough to captivate my adolescent midwestern imagination.

When I went to California for real, I was working for McDonnell Douglas Corporation (now Boeing) and was offered a promotion to Huntington Beach, located just south of Los Angeles. I'd spent my entire life in St. Louis, including college, and I couldn't wait to leave and see the Arch in my rearview mirror.

Overall, I enjoyed my time in California, although I worked a lot and travelled for business. I either didn't take the time or have the time to fully experience the "California " lifestyle... but the weather was nice. I grew to like the beach in the winter when it wasn't crowded and hiking in nearby mountains. But a couple of earthquakes gave me a jolt.

I eventually married my girlfriend from St. Louis, and after a wedding in the depth of a midwest winter, we packed up a U-Haul and headed west again.

For young married twenty-somethings, it was a carefree life in Huntington Beach. We settled in a comfortable two-bedroom apartment not far from work and spent time going to the beach, camping and enjoying what my wife called the "shopping mall weather. "

We moved after a couple of years because we started having kids and our apartment a mile from the beach became cramped. The only house I could afford then was a two-bedroom attached townhouse in the desert an hour-and-a-half drive from work.

The morning we left for good, on an airplane, there was an earthquake. It was probably a good time to leave the California dream behind.

So I'm happy for my sister, who has embraced the west coast lifestyle.

I'll have to go see her some time; California is a nice place to visit.

A CRADLE CARDINAL

I guess you can call me a "cradle Cardinal" fan.

There is a saying; whatever baseball team was "yours" when you were 10 years old, they're still your team, no matter where you might live or how old you get.

My Cardinals were Bob Gibson, Lou Brock, Curt Flood and the 1968 World Series loss to the Tigers. I was born in St. Louis and started following the team when I was, oh, about six years old.

There is some Cardinal baseball DNA in my blood. While my dad is from Brooklyn, and followed the Dodgers,my Mom is from Jefferson City. Her dad was part of the regional "Cardinal nation" that grew up throughout the Midwest and west when the Cardinals were the baseball team farthest west and KMOX radio beamed games to 48 states. Though I didn't know my grandfather, my grandmother used to tell me he "lived and died" with the Cardinals.

But one thing I'd never experienced until a couple of weeks ago was the Cardinal "Winter Warmup," an annual gathering of the faithful held downtown each January.

As a "cradle" fan, honestly, the Warmup didn't really appeal to me.

I figured it was for all of those out-state, small-town Cardinal fans who flocked here for a glimpse of their heroes and to buy up assorted Cardinal paraphernalia.

But myself? I'm a St. Louisan who can read and hear about the team everyday, patiently waiting until April when they will take up residence in my town for 81 games.

I don't buy tickets; I only go to games when someone offers me a seat. I don't have cable, so I don't watch many games on TV. I just quietly follow the team day-to-day, listening to the radio, charting their course through the six months of baseball summer. Like all fans, I suspend disbelief when it comes to the huge salaries and drug use. Is it a business? Is it a game? Broadcaster Bob Costas once said: "Neither, dummy, it's both." I'll stick with the game part.

All of my worldly sophistication changed last year when I discovered a rabid baseball fan in my house — Theresa, my six-year-old daughter.

I have six kids older than Theresa, including five boys, and while a couple of them follow the team, none of them caught the baseball bug like I had. A couple of my sons played ball for a while, but when I would say to them in the middle of July, "Geez, can you believe we only got three hits last night off of (some nameless pitcher from the Pirates)," they'd say, "Oh really?" and go back to whatever they were doing. Unlike myself at their ages, they weren't grabbing the sports page when the morning paper came, checking box scores and figuring out "how many games out" we were in the standings versus how many left to play. Or whether the wind would be blowing in or out at Wrigley Field during the upcoming weekend series in Chicago.

But at some point during last year's championship season, I realized that I could "talk baseball" with Theresa. I think her defining moment was the Sunday in July that we got some last-minute tickets and she went with her mother to a game and saw Albert Pujols hit three home runs. Unlike other kids at her age who I brought to games, she didn't squirm in her seat, waiting for a chance to buy cotton candy or to walk around.

As last season drew to a close and the team moved precariously towards the playoffs, I began to wonder about my young daughter's interest in baseball. It made sense in different ways. First, she was one of the more athletic of my kids. While most of my kids play or have played grade school soccer and some other sports, it was for them mostly for fun. Kids like these generally leave organized sports by the time they reach high school, which is fine, and my kids have gravitated toward music and other indoor extra-curriculars.

But Theresa is always moving around, wanting to play catch or play outside. And at an early age she could throw a baseball harder and straighter than some of her older siblings.

Since I'm not a natural athlete, although I played some high school sports, I figured Theresa had inherited her desire from some other part of the family. And it made sense that baseball, with its handsome young players and graceful movements, appealed to her.

As the Cardinals barely reached the playoffs and began their amazing run to the World Series, I found myself in my excitement telling others about Theresa's interest. It was kind of cute to tell them that my six-year-old girl was a "big fan."

One day, I was explaining this to someone, wondering aloud why Theresa was so interested in baseball.

"Well that's simple," she said. "It's her connection to you."

Huh? In true "duh" moment fashion, it took awhile for this to sink in.

I have a lot of kids, and my wife and I are always talking about how we try to make time to do something special with each one. But the practical fact is that when you do have time, it's generally a group activity. And since I tend to naturally understand boys better, I can see how Theresa might sometimes be overlooked.

So she and I went down together to the Winter Warmup. We took pictures of Albert Pujols and David Eckstein. She hit balls in the kids batting cage and threw a few pitches to a plastic catcher. We picked up a bag full of mostly free mementos. And of course, we got a picture with Fredbird.

As an adult, I probably wouldn't have been compelled to go myself to the Warmup. Because of the World Series win, the event was sold out, and at times there were so many people you could barely move, the autograph lines were long, and the trinket-sellers were jammed into every corner of the exhibition hall. But if you're a young fan, it was — like the Cardinals slogan says — "baseball heaven."

Meanwhile, my daughter keeps asking me if the team "has signed Jeff Weaver yet" and when spring training starts.

So for those who care: pitchers and catchers report to Jupiter, Florida, on Valentine's Day, February 14.

LIVING THE 'GREEN' LIFE

Do you have "eco-anxiety"?

A couple of weeks ago, Terri Reilly, head of the St. Louis Earth Day celebration, came to visit. Reilly has turned a small, localized "hippie" event into a broad-based, community-wide "happening." It includes not only the Mom-and-Pop hemp-growers, but some of the city's largest corporations. It will be held again this year in Forest Park on the grounds of the Muny Opera.

Yes, "green" is the buzzword of the day, but it also makes economic sense for business, she said. She's slowly working on some of the city's largest entertainment venues and encouraging them to recycle; the St. Louis Cardinals are recycling this year at the new Busch Stadium and hopefully soon the St. Louis Rams and the St. Louis Convention Center will also.

Anyway, Reilly talked about a meeting she attended. She was walking into the building and she saw an empty beer can and picked it up. Without thinking, she walked into the meeting with the beer can. She realized too late that it might not be the best thing to carry into a morning gathering.

"I thought, O.K., I can't worry about it. I was having my own 'eco-anxiety' attack," she said.

Loosely defined, the term refers to some people's hyper-awareness of the environment. Should I really throw this piece of paper away? Does my car get enough gas mileage? Is this piece of plastic with the number '6' on the bottom something I should put in the recycling bin? Am I creating too much carbon dioxide when I exhale? (Alright, I made that one up…).

I understand the anxiety. I have a son who is an environmental science major in college. He's my "eco-son." His influence — along with my wife's inability to throw anything away that might possibly be used again — has created our own "green" household paranoia.

To feel better, I did my own family's inventory of our efforts to "reduce, reuse and recycle."

• Luckily, our neighborhood is part of the city's curbside recycling program, which is great. They take cans, bottles and paper. We also save cardboard, but that has to go to the recycling center on Kingshighway Boulevard and I-44. When I take old boxes there, I realize how lucky we are… many of the other people have to carry all of their recyclables and manually separate them.

• Even though I helped my son do a science fair project on composting, I'm still not sure how it works. Biology was not my strongest subject in school. All I know is that any food waste we have that doesn't contain meat, I carry out and throw on a big brown pile of dirt in the backyard. The pile never seems to grow; in fact it shrinks. My eco-son says the micro-organisms are turning the apple peels and egg shells into rich black dirt. I still think it has something to do with the growing crowd of possums and rabbits in our backyard looking for a snack.

• This is where it gets a little weird. I've gotten used to my wife's "dumpster diving" habits, cruising city alleys around our house, looking for discarded furniture and even clothing.

But last fall, I noticed my high school son had stopped making his lunch in the morning for school. I thought: either he's not eating or he's spending his own money in the cafeteria. Turns out, he's, well, "mooching." Asking people if there's anything they don't want to eat... he'll take it. He said it's amazing what kids will throw away — grapes, sandwiches, even chips. He also stations himself near the trash cans, grabbing cans and bottles before they go into the trash. The recycling bin is just ten feet away, he says. Once my son explained what he was doing, I thought: oh great, I'll be getting a call from some school administrator. But when I asked one teacher about it, he said it was no big deal; "We have a lot of eccentric kids at our school." When I realized my son was doing it out of a desire to reduce waste — and not just because we have too many vegetables in our refrigerator — I didn't worry about it.

Not long after learning this, my eco-son told me about "freegans." You've heard the term "vegan." These are super-vegetarians who don't eat meat, dairy, eggs, or any animal products. Freegans aren't so picky; they get *all* of their meals from the trash.

I realize that homeless people pick through the trash for food, and God bless them. But somehow my middle-class sensibilities would cause me to shudder if my kids start picking through the dumpsters for food.

Now *that* would give me eco-anxiety.

WILL YOU BE MY FB FRIEND?

I have 14 friends.

How many do you have?

That's according to my Facebook page, which I warily joined a few weeks ago.

It's not that I'm anti-technology, it's just that I'm at a "certain age" where the internet has a limited appeal. Email is great; websites, Google, no problem; Wikipedia — well, OK, I do have a problem with that — but like all technology it's just a tool, and it's how you use it that matters.

For the past year, I've gotten occasional e-mails from people I didn't know very well asking me to be their "friend" and join Facebook. I ignored them. I knew Facebook and MySpace only as something teenagers used to "network" with friends. I knew that I didn't want my pre-teen kids to use it, and the case of that St. Charles MySpace hoax and the tragic teen suicide of Megan Meier made me even more wary.

Finally, a couple of weeks ago, two people I know in business asked me to be their "friend." They weren't people I talked to frequently — maybe once a year — but they were important people to my business and I didn't want to ignore them.

So I joined.

After registering, I was asked to create my "profile" and fill out information about myself. Since I didn't really intend to use it much, I kept it simple… hometown, schools I attended, my job. I did not, for instance, feel the need to list my political or religious views or what I was "looking for" in a relationship.

I was compelled, however, to post a photograph. If I hadn't, my profile would have appeared with a silly-looking silhouette. I picked a photo of myself with my sister when I was about eight years old. Hello, Facebook world, it's me!

I still don't get it, but the appeal of Facebook is to show the world an image of yourself. How many friends you have, what kind of music you like, and what you're doing this weekend. It's clearly geared to socially-concious teenagers. That's fine, but for a middle-aged married guy, I don't see a lot of use for it.

Except… if you have teenagers.

Facebook let me know that I could ask to be "friends" with four of my kids. One is out of college, two are in college, and one is in high school. Now I was starting to get interested. So I sent them messages… could I be their "friend"?

What I found, like millions of other parents, is that you can glimpse how your kids present themselves to others on Facebook. But it seems a little voyeuristic and perhaps privacy-invading, like snooping around in their rooms.

One of my kids seemed upset — like I *was* snooping into their social world or checking up on them. Yes it was interesting to see what their "favorite saying" was but most of it didn't interest me, especially a feature of Facebook called the "wall."

The "wall" is a posting on the page where any of your friends can put a message. Which means any of your friends can see a personal message to you from someone else.

This might be useful for say, letting people know about an event you're attending, but why write something like, "Hey, what's up?"

How could a message like that possibly interest anyone else? Why not just e-mail — or, yes, even make a phone call — to tell your friend "what's up"? Plus, if someone posts a message on your wall, you get an e-mail telling you that. Why don't they just send *you* an email?

To me, it's like text-messaging, another thing I don't get… why don't you just call them? Have we become so busy or conversation-avoidant that we use our telephone *not* to talk?

I shouldn't knock Facebook. It has 90 million members worldwide and it is trying to expand beyond its initial core group of college students. It is trying to tap into the career world and baby boomers like myself to join the "social network." One way it does this is to help you connect with old classmates. A couple of people who asked to be my "friends" are people I didn't know well in school. One I don't remember at all. Another one I never liked.

Oops! I have to go… I just got an e-mail from Facebook. I have another friend!

That's 15 now. Hi, Alice!

HOOP DREAMS

"It's the most wonderful time of the year."

Sure, the holidays are nice, but for me, this is the best: the time of musty old gyms, loud buzzers and middle-aged knees pounding on hard tile floors.

Basketball season.

Last Thursday night at 6 p.m. I found myself in south St. Louis at St. Margaret of Scotland's gym. The reason? The second round of the 7th grade boys holiday basketball tournament. My son Danny plays on the Cathedral School team, and I serve as the team's manager.

Long ago, a wise grade-school parent told me: never be coach. Be assistant coach, or manager, but get someone else for the top job. Then you'll never have to figure out those pesky rules or deal with a parent who thinks their kid should play more. Danny's team has two coaches. I just make the phone calls, set up the practices and hope the other two coaches are never sick for a game. If I were to coach, I don't know who'd be more frightened at the prospect: me or them.

Anyway, Danny's team played a close game and eventually won to go to the finals of the tournament. After the game I dashed home, got on my own basketball clothes and went up to a neighborhood gym to play with a group of guys on our regular Thursday night pick-up game.

I haven't always had a great affinity for the sport. As a kid, I had some interest but little talent. But the summer before high school I grew six inches and suddenly I was among the taller kids in my class. My father encouraged me to play and I even went to a week-long basketball camp in Belleville.

I barely made the team (third string) my freshman year and my best position was playing the smart-aleck at the end of the bench. That year, one of the more embarassing things in my young life happened. We had driven to another school for a game, and as we dressed, our team's star player realized he 'd left his jersey at school. The coach, who didn't like me (the feeling was mutual), told me to give the star player my jersey and for me to sit in the stands.

I actually wasn't that upset; I figured I could walk around and go to the snack bar during the game. There was little chance I'd play anyway. Luckily, there was another teacher from school with our team, and when he heard what happened, he hopped in his car and retrieved the star player's jersey just in time for the game. This made the coach like me even less and I rode the bench the rest of the year.

I played again sophomore year, had a better coach, but that was my last year because I knew I couldn't make the varsity team.

I didn't play basketball again for 20 years after that. It began a few years ago with a backyard group of guys on our street and we played occasionally in the spring and fall. I started to really enjoy it and I organized the Thursday night game.

We play in a grade school gym with hard, slick, tile floors. Other than the "regulars," the guys who show up seem to get younger and quicker and I have to play extremely well to keep up.

Once again, except for an occasional night, I'm among the least talented players. But now, unlike high school, I know I'll always be able to play and not sit out a game.

Why? They have to let me play. I have the key to the gym.

LOSING SLEEP WRITING THIS COLUMN

I lost sleep writing this column.

Actually, it doesn't take much for me to lose sleep. Like a recent *Newsweek* cover about how little and how poorly Americans are sleeping points out, we're overloaded with stress, worry and responsibility.

But that's not my problem; I'm just a light sleeper.

I could spend $1,000 on one of those high-tech beds ("What's your sleep number?"), but it won't matter to me if it's filled with air, water or some NASA anti-friction material. If there's a creak in some far corner of my old house at three in the morning, I'll probably hear it.

But really, this isn't about me. Since my favorite insomniac pastime is listening to an old transistor radio with an earpiece, I thought I'd give the sleeping public an amateur critique of the sometimes strange and sometimes compelling fare on midnight radio.

KWMU (National Public Radio affiliate): At some point late each evening, KWMU switches to British Broadcasting. It's a great alternative to our daily dose of America-centered news. On the hourly newscast, it might take three or four stories before the U.S. is mentioned. You'll hear what's happening in Zimbabwe, Croatia and London, all delivered in a clipped British accent. There are global feature stories, too; rambling National Public Radio-type pieces about, say, weather patterns in Turkey or the plight of refugees in Outer Mongolia. Sports stories are primarily about soccer and cricket, complete with standings, schedules, and sports clichés with a foreign twist: we bloody gave 110 per cent today.

Alistair Cooke gives a melancholy "Letter from America" periodically, and each night there is a reading from classic literature, such as an hour of *Catch-22*.

KDHX: After midnight, I'm not much for listening to music — maybe I like the sound of a voice — but for a change of pace I'll switch to the community radio station KDHX. Like Forrest Gump said, you never know what you're going to get, from loud garage punk rock to easy-listening love songs. The announcers are usually entertaining. Free from the constraints of a commercial station (and a paycheck), these volunteers give up their early morning sleep to share their musical obsession with listeners. But not always. One morning I tuned in to hear an animated group of 20-somethings chatting away for a half-hour like they had just left a club on Washington Avenue, oblivious to the fact that they were supposed to be playing music.

KMOX: The old warhorse "Voice of St. Louis" features John Carney until 2 a.m. Carney, son of KMOX legend Jack Carney, brings a refreshing change to the station's rigid, conservative, "crabby old man" format. Carney is funny, breezy, has interesting guests, and isn't afraid to tweak the station's status quo. The late KMOX radio czar Bob Hyland surely did some grave-turning when Carney interviewed singer Robert Plant and played "Stairway to Heaven." After Carney, though, KMOX returns to AARP programming.

KTRS: The strangest thing you'll hear through the night is *Coast to Coast A.M.*, a nationally syndicated show hosted by St. Louisan George Noory. Noory, known as the ***Nighthawk*** on KTRS, inherited the show from founder Art Bell. Bell was — and probably still is — a certified U.F.O. conspiracy theorist who sees black helicopters over every hillside. Tune in and you'll hear experts on alien abduction, the Tri-Lateral Commission and callers talking about near-death experiences. Noory, a longtime St. Louis television producer, is trying to expand the subject matter (and plausibility) of the show, but he still gets callers who claim they're channeling the voice of their ancestors.

How can you sleep through that?

TOO OLD TO ROCK 'N ROLL

Acoustic/electric guitar: $300
Guitar amplifier: $150
Singing lessons: $80
Amount paid to me for first "gig": $25

There's a joke about a mother who walks into a room and her son is singing. "What did you do with that money?" she asks her son. "What money?" the kid replies. "The money I gave you for singing lessons."

One Saturday in July I packed up my 1993 Nissan Altima with a guitar, amplifier, assorted paraphernelia and two kids and drove more than two hours to Jefferson City. Outside of town, at someone's weekend cabin on the Osage River, six other people and I set up our equipment and played music for two hours to a half-interested birthday party of about 50 people. It was probably the hottest day of the year (between sets we cooled off in the river) and at the end, there were about four people left listening. These included my two kids (who couldn't leave), the owner of the house (who lived there) and a drunk neighbor who whooped enthusiastically after each song. For that I got $25 and a new title: paid musician.

That's not to say that we weren't any good; in fact, I thought we sounded great. These are guys (and one wife) who've played together for decades, but mostly just in a basement or garage. They've always taken it seriously.... serious fun, that is.

My mid-life musical odyssey began about a year and half ago, when Dave Swope called me out of the blue. He was one of the guys in the band whom I knew from high school. I hadn't heard from him in twenty years. While he and a group had continued playing together off and on all these years, I'd been playing mostly to myself or to the squirrels on our third floor.

He invited me to come to one of their "jam" sessions. It was fun, although I was clearly not quite up to their level of playing. It got more comfortable the more we played and then this "gig" opportunity came up.

We decided that if it went well, we'd try to play three or four times a year at parties. With three of the seven living out of town (Cape Girardeau and Jefferson City) and all of us with families, careers, etc., that seemed like a good enough plan.

I've joked with my wife that the band is cheaper than a cherry red convertible. If this is a mid-life crisis, then it's not so bad. After all, it's just four or five guys in a basement in south county. I can't get into too much trouble. I've since talked to a couple of guys my age or older who have done the same thing. One is a commercial real estate broker. Another is a photographer. In each case they hooked up with old high school friends and started playing again.

The best thing is that no one has any illusions about what this is. Twenty years ago, we might have harbored illusions of fame and fortune, but now we're glad to squeeze in some practice time once a month between our kids' soccer games.

Our career highlight was a couple of years ago when we played in a south St. Louis bar called *Colorado Bob's* (it has nothing to do with Colorado, it's on Macklind, and has a sailboat out front). Due to a series of coincidences too complicated to explain here, on the same night we played two guys from a semi-popular band in the 1970s showed up. The band was called Poco, a country-rock group that was similar to the Eagles… except for the million-selling albums. Still, they had several top-40 songs, including one named *Call it Love*. The two Poco guys came up to our stage and played that song. And I played along. Cool.

Anyway, some guys go fishing. Some guys golf. Some guys put on a guitar and pound on drums and sing old Chuck Berry songs. What's it worth, anyway?

Chance to play and sing in a band: priceless.

TURNING 40: "GEEZER ROCK"

In a couple of weeks, on the night I turn 40, I'll go to the Riverport Amphitheater to see my final rock concert. My oldest son is planning to go with me. It will be his first.

I long ago gave up going to big concerts. I've only been to two at Riverport, both of which were to see Jimmy Buffett. But that's hardly a "rock" concert — more like a Carribean frat-party for grown-ups in arrested development.

The live music I see now is usually in smaller, quieter, smoke-free confines like The Sheldon or an occasional street fair.

But when I saw the ad for this concert, several factors moved me to pay exorbitant ticket prices to travel long distances (anything west of I-270) and battle road-rage traffic.

First were the groups. The opening act is Wilco, a country-rock band originally from the Belleville area which I like and I've never heard live before. The main band is R.E.M., which I've followed since they started in the early 1980s when I was in college.

The next factor was the timing with my 40th birthday. The thought of someone over that age going to a rock concert always seemed a bit pathetic to me.

Sure, the Rolling Stones are in their 50s and summer amphitheaters are filled with all the other baby boomer bands — "geezer rock," it's called. But maybe it was the Grateful Dead concert I went to in the early 1980s that convinced me. Aging hippies with grey ponytails and tie-dye shirts twirled around in the aisles and I thought: that's too old. Enjoy the music, but *please*, in the privacy of your own home. "Rock" music is supposed to be about youth, rebellion and a lack of mortgage payments.

Finally was the intriguing prospect of going to a concert with my son. While most of his music doesn't intersect mine, R.E.M. is an exception. They were one of the first of the so-called "alternative" bands and they are still played on the radio stations my 14-year-old listens to. But the fact that he is going (and that he knows all the words to R.E.M's song *It's the End of the World As We Know It*) is a little unnerving.

I went to my first concert when I was 13 with my two older brothers and their friends. It was the Beach Boys at Kiel Opera House. No way in the world could I imagine my father — a buttoned-down bank officer at the time — taking me along.

So I'll go, wear earplugs, and marvel at the sea of youth around me. The next morning, as my wife jokes, I'll probably develop a sudden affinity for Big Band music. And my son will wonder what I was doing there the night before.

"WE'LL ALWAYS HAVE PARIS..."

Last year around this time I was lying on my favorite couch in our living room, at a time somewhere between waking up and getting the kids ready. It's one time of the day when I have a few minutes to read the newspaper. In terms of consciousness, I'm right above "coma," heading for "able to operate heavy machinery" – like driving the kids to school.

As I flipped through the paper, I stopped at a full-page ad from TWA. It was one of those "big specials" they run periodically: $250 for a round trip ticket to Paris. Of course, it said "tickets are limited," and there was a list of restrictions, but instead of moving on to the next page of the paper, I stopped.

Why not? I thought as my mind raced. Why not surprise my wife for Valentine's Day with tickets to Paris?

It did hold a special attraction to me. When I was 21, just graduated from college, I went to France to visit my future wife. It was a trip I'd planned and saved for – my first (and only) trip abroad. I knew that when I returned, I would start "real life," in this case a $175-a-week job as a reporter for the *Belleville Journal* newspaper.

For three weeks, I traveled through France with Laura and her European friends. I "saw the sights," in big towns and small, got little sleep riding trains on a Eurail pass and had a great time…especially knowing I would soon be home writing about school board meetings and church socials.

Meanwhile, back on my couch, I ticked off the problems with going back to France. First – the money. Would my credit card hold it? If not, could I get a higher limit, take out a loan, start moonlighting, sell a car…? Okay, I could get the money. Next: What about the kids? Could I farm them out to assorted grandparents and aunts and uncles for at least five days? Maybe – I would probably strain family relations in some cases, but hey, we were talking *Paris*. What about time off work? It's a busy time of year, but as long as no one quit, I could stand to get away for a while.

Then reality intruded. My "flight of fancy" crashed as soon as one of my kids said, "Dad, get up. We'll be late for school." There were just too many obstacles. I realized the next time I would get to France with my wife would probably be with a "seasoned citizens" tour sponsored by the AARP.

So, on Valentine's Day, as we've done for several years, after a family dinner, we pulled out the slide projector. It's the one time of year we actually look through trays of slides from past family vacations. But we always go through the slides from the trip to France 20 years ago, so, in a sense, we did get to Paris for a while.

Sure, it wasn't on a plane, but I did get to watch from my couch.

WATCHIN' THE WB NETWORK

"I made my family disappear."

That line is from a wide-eyed Macauley Caulkin in the movie, ***Home Alone***, when his family went to Paris and forgot to take him along.

On a recent Friday afternoon, I helped my family pack up a station wagon, I closed the back hatch, and watched them drive off to Colorado for spring break without me.

I had mixed emotions. My first thought was a déjà vu of my own family packing up an old Ford Country Squire station wagon (no fake wood paneling) and going to Colorado. Those were different times; no seat belts or car seats, and my Dad could drive 85 miles an hour with us five kids wrestling in the back without any concern about state troopers or car safety.

But this time I wasn't going with my family. The Colorado trip seemed like a good idea last fall when we realized our kids' spring breaks would match up and a friend offered their condo. My wife has family there and we have old friends from when we lived in Denver years ago.

But as March approached, it became clear why we had never done a big spring break trip with the kids; things were just too busy for me at work. And who would take care of our chickens for a whole week?

It's been 20 years since I was single and lived on my own, but every year or so, I get a few days or a week on my own at home.

It's a predictable pattern; the first few days are kind of fun and liberating, but then it starts to get a little, well, weird.

I realize that while I might complain that "I'm so busy" balancing life and work and family, the fact is that my family doesn't *keep* me from doing more, it actually helps. With less time to do stuff, I tend to get more done. The flip side of that theorem: give me unlimited time and, well, I'll stay up too late and watch bad t.v.

Day One. My son Dan from college was home the weekend my family took off, so I had dinner with him and his girlfriend and watched "March Madness" basketball. But I also found time to work on taxes and financial aid.

Day Two. It was nice having Dan around, but I realized that I could probably never live alone with this kid for too long. Why? We're too much alike. We're both a bit absent-minded. We went for a bike ride, but he got home first and had the only house key, and I pounded on the door for 20 minutes as he took a shower.

Day Three. After my productive day of finishing taxes and financial aid, Dan leaves to go back to college and things begin to slowly fall apart. I stay up too late watching bad t.v.

Day Four. My brother and sister-in-law ask me over for dinner. I get home at 9 p.m., but instead of doing work and going to bed, I stay up too late watching bad t.v. I fall asleep on the couch.

Day Five. I go to dinner with my parents, which is nice, but afterwards I stop at the Galleria to do some clothes shopping. I *never* go "clothes shopping." But I realize I'm running out of clean shirts so I get to Dillards at 9 p.m., they close at 9:30, and I buy new shoes, three shirts and a belt. The next morning, I realize two of the shirts are pink and one doesn't fit.

Day Six. I think I'm losing it now. When I get home from work, I feed the chickens and I find myself talking to to them. That's not necessarily weird, but then I wait for them to answer back, as if they actually know who I am. I then microwave a "Lean Cuisine," which I eat in front of the t.v. I have a mental list of things I "should do," including paying bills and starting to clean the house, but at 7 p.m. I find myself inexplicably drawn into a *really* bad t.v. drama on the "WB" network. For an hour I watch a melodramatic high school show called *One Tree Hill* about a "loser" who brings a gun to school and terrorizes all the "popular" kids in a hostage standoff. Worse, yet, even with the bad writing and Luke Perry hairdos, I *care* what happens. The episode ends with a cliffhanger.

Day Seven. My wife calls from Colorado and she proposes I meet her in Kansas City to surprise the kids and help them all get home. Despite the change in plans and added expense, I jump at the chance.

Day Eight. I meet my family at a Holiday Inn in Blue Springs, Missouri. It's great to see them. As I help unload, my wife informs me that one of the kids had been throwing up for the past hour. That night two more kids get stomach flu.

But that's OK. It's good to be back with the family, sick or not.

I just wonder if I'll remember to tune back in to *One Tree Hill* on Thursday night.

LIFE IN THE TIME OF PRESIDENT BUSH (2005)

Imagine a world where the U.S. President is an intellectually curious, principled leader. He believes in a strong defense and he won't negotiate with terrorists. His White House staff is a group of bright, articulate people who have their own opinions but always respect the wisdom of their boss.

The president agonizes over matters of life and death. He believes in equal opportunity and a strong educational system. He goes to church, but he doesn't believe it has any place in politics. He is in fact a former college professor, but he doesn't live in an ivory tower. He has a gift for communication, able to reach both the common man and foreign leaders. While he's principled, he also knows how far to compromise with the opposing party for legislation everyone can live with.

I want to live in *that* world.

I'm referring, of course, to the fictional world of *West Wing*, an NBC television show that chronicles the administration of President Jed Bartlet, played by actor Martin Sheen. I only watch two network television shows with any regularity. There's *West Wing* and *NYPD Blue*, which recently had its final show. So I'm left with the gang on *West Wing*.

Bartlet, a Democrat, is clearly in the mold of John F. Kennedy, the moderate Democrat who stood up to the Russians in Cuba, but also began the country's march toward civil rights in the early 1960s.

In the show, which recently had its season finale, Bartlet is nearing the end of his second term and headed for retirement while dealing with multiple sclerosis, a progressive disease.

In this alternate presidential universe, the season ends with two candidates poised to face off in the fall elections. Congressman Matt Santos, played by actor Jimmy Smits, is the Democratic candidate. He's a charismatic Hispanic who inspires passion, but can he attract voters beyond the party's traditional ethnic and liberal base?

His opponent is Republican Sen. Arnold Vinick, played by Alan Alda. Vinick is a moderate, John Danforth-kind of Republican. He's pro-business and hates taxes but doesn't go to church and can't quite stomach the right-wing moral-majority base of his party. He's the kind of Republican even a Democrat could respect.

And then I woke up in the *real* world.

My world is inhabited by a President who may be principled, but hardly anyone would call "intellectually curious." He avoided military service, yet starts a war on what many believe were unfounded claims. He doesn't negotiate with terrorists yet still can't find the one responsible for our country's worst terrorist incident. While he commendably agonizes over the lives of the unborn and those attached to feeding tubes, when he was governor of Texas he oversaw the highest number of death-penalty executions of any state in the Union.

His staff seems to be composed of morally righteous people who can't separate religion from the republic. Like Bartlet, he does have a gift for communication, but he seemingly would rather use the force of his majority to get his way rather than work out a compromise.

But it's not like the Democrats have stirring candidates in the real world. Last fall, Senator John Kerry, who faced the President in the election, was a John F. Kennedy-wannabe (war veteran, Massachusetts liberal) but lacked two traits: charisma and humility. The new leader of the national Democratic party, Howard Dean, has charisma, but "screamed" his way into losing the nomination last year when a long primary campaign exposed his brittle personality. And Democrats in Congress can be just as nasty, uncompromising and vindictive as Republicans when *they* hold the power.

We still have more than three long years before the next presidential election. That's plenty of time for both parties to come up with compelling, consensus-building candidates. In the meantime, pardon me if I vote to stay in the *West Wing* world.

Update: Barack Obama, a former college professor and a moderate, articulate Democrat with charisma and humility, is now president. But he inherited from President Bush two wars and the beginnings of an unprecedented economic crisis. So it's almost like the West Wing; *now we just need a Hollywood ending.*

ZEN AND THE ART OF WINDSHIELD REPAIR

Take your time. Have the right tools. Follow instructions.

That's the lesson from one of my favorite do-it-yourself manuals. No, it's not the *New York Times Guide to Home Renovation*, which I own, but rather a novel I read 20 years ago called *Zen and the Art of Motorcycle Maintenance.*

I don't remember much about the book except for the nine words that started this column.

Recently, I ignored that advice on an incredibly simple car repair job. It took twice as long, cost twice as much and caused enough frustration to send my blood pressure soaring.

As a cautionary tale to you do-it-yourselfers, please read carefully:

7:30 a.m. I wake up on a Wednesday. After eating breakfast and leisurely reading the paper, I remember that I had told my wife that I'd fix the rearview mirror in the family van, which had fallen from the inside of the windshield. Now, I'm not a car guy, but clearly this was in my limited repair ability.

8:15 a.m. I drive the two blocks to Reliance Automotive on Kingshighway. Mike, the attendant, has me buy a small repair kit with glue and instructions. Cost: $2.70. He tells me to make sure I remove the metal "button" in the mirror assembly and not to touch the glue after I've put it on the windshield. I joke, "I won't be back soon, I hope." Since I'm dressed in a tee-shirt, shorts, sandals, and just-awakened hair, he eyes me warily and probably figures me for what I am: a middle-aged car incompetent.

8:20 a.m. I get back home. I realize I'd better hurry to get it done to have time to get dressed and to work by 9 a.m. I grab a screwdriver and a scraper from the "auxiliary" tool set in the kitchen (in other words, tools that I was too lazy to bring bring back down to the basement tool bench). I also grab a rag to wipe off the windshield.

8:25 a.m. I try to pry the metal button off of the mirror. It won't budge. I realize I should have brought the assembly to the basement tool bench, put it into the vise, and lightly tapped the metal button with a hammer to get it out. To save time, I figure I'll just glue the whole mirror to the windshield.

8:30 a.m. My arm feels like it's about to fall off as I awkwardly try to hold still the rearview mirror to the windshield. Every time I let go, hoping it will stick, it falls down. Without thinking, I reach up to touch the glue to see if it's drying. Oops. What did Mike say? I painfully pull my finger off the hardening blob of glue.

8:35 a.m. I run down to the basement tool bench, put the mirror into the vise, and lightly tap the metal button with a hammer. It comes out. I sprint back to the car, hoping the glue hasn't completely dried. It hasn't! I stick the button on the windshield and go back in to change for work.

8:47 a.m. I check the mirror button before I leave for work. It is glued firmly to the windshield. Great! I try to attach the mirror and realize that in my rush, I glued the wrong side to the windshield. I try to pry it off, but it's set. This is a critical moment: my wife is standing at the door with kids, ready to leave in the van. Do I just go to work and fix it later? But I said I'd fix it; do I want my wife and children driving another half-day in a dangerous vehicle? Hey, I'm the great provider, the hunter-gatherer, I need to protect my family. I decide to fix it now. I tell my wife it'll be just a few minutes. Just then my next-door neighbor, Steve Gray, goes out on his front porch and says "hi" to me. Oh no, I think. Steve is an engineer and home-improvement master who has single-handedly rebuilt the interior and most of the exterior of his 100-plus year-old home. I hope he doesn't ask good-naturedly, "Whatcha doin'?" or "Need some help?" If he does, I could lie and say, "I thought I'd start on that new addition in the back today," but he must sense I don't want to be bothered and he doesn't ask. Steve's a sensitive guy.

8:52 a.m. Back at Reliance. Mike doesn't look surprised to see me again. I ask him could I just buy another metal button, glue it to the one I just glued incorrectly on the windshield, and be done with it? He shakes his head, clearly disappointed with me. "But the button is set!" I say. He tells me to use some nail polish remover and a Q-Tip to loosen the glue and then pry it off. He's obviously seen my type before.

8:58 a.m. The great hunter-gatherer has to go to his wife and ask for some nail polish remover. She sees the mood I'm in and kindly doesn't comment. Armed with my manly tools I start dousing the metal button with nail polish remover. Nothing happens at first, except the van fills with toxic and head-lightening fumes. I gasp and open the window. Finally, the metal button starts to loosen and it falls off the windshield, with no visible scars on the glass.

9:06 a.m. I take a deep breath and start over. I take my time. I use the right tools. I read the instructions on the tiny adhesive package. It works! My wife drives off in a safe vehicle and I get to work late, but at least I feel like I've mastered the mystery of the car mirror button.

Lesson learned? Don't mess with Zen.

SUNFLOWER HOUSE (1999)

Nineteen-ninety-nine was the year I turned 40, the year my mom nearly died, the year my youngest sprang from his diapers... and the last year of the century. But mostly, it was the year of the sunflower house.

* * *

I was munching on pretzels in our kitchen in January when my wife told me she was going to grow a sunflower house in our backyard that summer.

A what?

While I've gotten used to Laura's garden preparations in the winter — seed catalogs in the mail and tiny pots on the windowsill— I was surprised about the sunflower house. I envisioned some kind of playground contraption. Some assembly certainly would be required.

In February, one day at work, my brother called to say our mother had experienced a heart "event" while vacationing in Hilton Head Island. The next morning tests showed blockage in five places. She was rushed to a hospital for an emergency five-way heart bypass operation. Two days later I stood next to her hospital bed, wondering how an energetic, athletic, 66-year-old woman could look so frail.

* * *

Later that month the sunflower house "kit" came and it was just a packet of seeds. The picture on the packet showed a square row of symmetrically perfect sunflowers, about eight feet tall. The sunflowers actually bent inward, creating a roof. An opening was left for the door.

I was skeptical. The sunflower house looked a bit contrived. Sure, it might grow in a climate-controlled greenhouse, but what about in our kid-trampled backyard? My wife is a good gardener but I doubted we could grow anything that healthy-looking in our tough city soil.

One May afternoon, I helped plant the house. With a spade, we dug three parallel trenches two inches deep in a square with six-foot long sides.

Within a week, right on cue, a series of small sunflower plants popped up in three neat little rows.

In late June we went on vacation and when we pulled up in front of the house after an 850-mile drive, everybody ran to the back yard to see how high they'd grown.

The plants kept growing, tall and straight like the ad said. The kids would periodically play in the house. By early August, some were taller than me and we began to look for the buds that would turn into flowers. By mid-August the first sunflowers bloomed and soon it was filled with colorful flowers. The tallest reached 12 feet high. The sunflower house also brought other visitors — large bumblebees, goldfinches and even a hummingbird.

* * *

On Aug. 19 I turned 40. That night I went to a rock concert featuring R.E.M.; I joked that it was my last rock concert and my oldest son's first — he came with us. I felt a little self-conscious, at my age, attending the concert, until I looked around. From teen-agers to 50-year-olds were in the audience. The most amazing thing? That the musical tastes of my son and I somehow intersected, at least for one night.

At summer's end the sunflower house started to slowly come apart. The huge flowers dried and the plants, top-heavy with seeds, fell over.

In early September, my oldest son started high school at St. Louis University High School. When he was in grade school, some days it seemed his matriculation would never end. But now it's shocking that in only four years he'll be gone. When he was a toddler, I used to tell Laura that some day he'd fill the doorway. That day is here.

Meanwhile, my youngest son shed his diapers and started pre-school. Doing the math, I figured we had used over 20,000 cloth and disposable diapers with all six kids. Getting him out of the diapers wasn't nearly as hard as realizing that he didn't need them — or us — as much.

* * *

In November we let the kids tear down the remaining stalks of the sunflower house. They gleefully ripped them out of the ground and promptly turned them into weapons, throwing them like spears. "Don't hit your sister" was about all I could say.

As they played, I looked over the bare patch of ground, just a few seeds left for the possums and birds to pick over. I began to wonder if any would sprout in the spring.

* * *

By the way, my mother is fine. She's back in Hilton Head on vacation, stronger than ever after her surgery. My wife said one reason she likes sunflowers so much is what they represent. In flower "lingo," sunflowers are a symbol of gratitude. I'm a believer now.

Update: ten years after I wrote this piece, my Mom fell down a set of stairs. She had emergency brain surgery, and thanks to an experienced surgeon (and blessedly good timing), she recovered nearly completely. She's back in Hilton Head again, and the residual effects of the fall are a half-moon shaped scar on her scalp and a slight limp from a healing broken foot. It might be time to plant another sunflower house.

CHICKEN JOURNAL:

BEWARE OF THE CHICKEN FLU?

A couple of weeks ago, a persistent little virus ran its course through our household, claiming all but my wife and youngest child. Its symptoms included high fever, nausea and a couple of days in bed.

It seems most colds and viruses strike us in the winter, when the kids are in school. A summer virus seemed odd. One night, my wife asked me to do a couple of chores before bed, including taking out the trash. "And don't forget to coop up the chickens," she called out.

As I walked by the chicken coop, I had a thought… nah. Couldn't be.

I'd heard a story recently on National Public Radio about "avian flu." I'm not prone to paranoia, but I suddenly had a vision of federal disease control workers in moon suits sealing off my backyard, carrying away poor Scarlet, Chicken Jane, Fluffy and Samantha (our chickens) like ET in the movie. Headlines the next day would scream: "Urban 'Clampetts' Likely Cause of Feathered Flu."

Granted, our hens were bought at Soulard Market, and we're half a world away from the reported cases of the avian flu, but hey…. if the north pole can melt and the government can tap our phones, I guess anything's possible.

At least that's what some people in a nearby suburb, University City, think. About the chickens, I mean.

In case you missed it, there have been quite a few ruffled feathers (sorry) about the city's proposal to allow U. City residents to keep chickens.

This started about a year ago, when the city council, after urging from chicken-fanciers, introduced an ordinance to allow residents to keep chickens. It was a pilot program and it was a model of municipal restraint: residents could keep up to seven hens (no roosters) as pets in their backyard and twice a year inspectors would make sure the chickens were in a healthy environment. Nearby communities like Clayton and Webster Groves had similar statutes.

No big deal, right?

Wrong. Just ask University City councilman Bob Wagner.

"We got a number of complaints when the pilot program was over," said Wagner. "Most of them were the we-don't-want-chickens-running-around variety. But some people mentioned the possibility of a pandemic from avian flu."

In fact, at a recent council meeting, one University City resident expressed concern about the H5N1 virus, the avian flu strain that is currently causing concern. "It could spark one of the deadliest epidemics the world has ever seen," the resident said, who urged termination of the pilot program.

Wagner, who spoke with the resigned wisdom of a village politician used to resolving petty disputes, wasn't necessarily critical of the chicken opponents. "I just wish some of them had read the ordinance, which addressed a lot of their concerns.

"I think it was more of a gut reaction. There was an implication that having chickens was too 'rural' for our community."

Wagner said that during the pilot program, only two residents applied for permits and there were no complaints (and I assume the permit-holders successfully passed their visits from the Chicken Inspectors). But when it came time to renew the pilot program in the spring, Wagner said the issue became a lightning rod during a heated mayoral battle. So, to appease the complainants, a number of items were added to the ordinance, including requiring *four* inspections a year and assessing a fine for non-permit-holding chicken keepers. Also, a moratorium on future permits was established.

Meanwhile, down here in the Central West End, things are a bit looser.

Before moving here 14 years ago, we lived in University City and we loved the community. Although when we moved we were more interested in getting a bigger house for raising kids rather than chickens, now having the birds has become now an unintended benefit of city living.

We've had chickens for two years now, and before we started we were told about a city ordinance that requires no more than four chickens (and no roosters). So we've stayed within the law (although we also have a parakeet, if that counts). But we've never heard from a Chicken Inspector.

Although I wasn't exactly enthusiastic when my wife and kids first talked about getting chickens — we already have enough living things in our household, known and unknown — I've since become a proponent. Other than cleaning the coop regularly, the birds are very low maintenance. They don't ask for much, other than shelter, food and water, and are pretty good pets. Not being the sharpest tools in the shed, they don't demand much attention (or necessarily remember who we are). But they are fun for the kids to hold and they have to be the only pet in the world which actually *produces* something useful for their owners. Four fresh eggs a day.

So as a former University City resident and a chicken keeper, I would like to assure their good citizens that they have nothing to fear by allowing chickens. Okay, so it *is* a bit "rural" but there's no moratorium against banjo players, right?

But just in case… maybe I better get a flu shot this fall.

SECTION VI
Trouble Right Here (City Living)

BARACK OBAMA SLEPT HERE

I recently drove by Barack Obama's house.

But he wasn't home.

Actually, I was with 50 other people on a bus tour of the south-side Chicago neighborhood called Hyde Park. My wife and two of my children had driven there in October for "parent's weekend" for our daughter, who is a freshman in college at the University of Chicago (UC).

The bus tour was free and meant we could sit for an hour, so we welcomed it. What was amazing was how similar Hyde Park is to where I live — except that it's a lot bigger and, well, no presidential candidate lives here.

The first similarity was the school's setting.

UC is a private, ivy-covered "urban" university, much like our own Washington University (WU). Like WU, it has a challenging academic curriculum and likes to think of itself as "midwestern Ivy League." Tuition at UC is also very expensive like WU, and thankfully it has a large endowment and very generous financial aid for "highly motivated" students like my daughter.

Depending on which direction you drive from the campus, you have to be careful. Go too far south or west of Hyde Park, and the neighborhood takes a definite "bad turn;" while WU is cradled by inner suburbs like Clayton and Richmond Heights, it's not far from some of the tougher areas of the city.

Just north of the UC campus is a neighborhood of big houses that were built in the second half of the 19th century by Paul Cornell, whose first cousin founded Cornell University.

Cornell developed the marshy land just west of Lake Michigan, creating estates for the titans of Chicago industry, including William Rand of the Rand McNally Map Company, Martin Ryerson, the lumber merchant, Gustavus Swift, the meatpacker, and Julius Rosenwald, the CEO of Sears, Roebuck & Co.

Like Julius Pitzman, who created the private streets of the CWE in St. Louis in the same time period, Cornell hoped to create an island of wealth and prestige on a train line far from the smoky industrial city. John D. Rockefeller, the oil magnate, established UC on a tract of land donated by Marshall Field, the department store owner.

It also attracted the most prominent architects of its day, including Frank Lloyd Wright and Eero Saarinen. Literary figures who lived in the area included Saul Bellow and Kurt Vonnegut, who attended UC.

The area, like our West End, went through several decades of "white flight" and neglect after World War II. In the 1960s and 1970s, urban pioneers came back to the area, starting to build the diverse community it is today.

Key to the development was the high quality of housing stock. Like the 100-year-old-plus mansions on Portland, Westmoreland and Kingsbury places in the CWE, Chicago's Hyde Park homes were bought by young UC professors, professionals and upwardly mobile African Americans. As a result, by the 1970s and 1980s, there were a number of newly prominent residents such as Lewis Farrakahn, Mohammed Ali, Carol Mosely Braun and eventually, Barack Obama, who built his political base there. Here in St. Louis, the CWE boasted famous residents from old-time business magnates Dwight Davis and Albert Lambert, literary figures T.S. Eliot and William Burroughs, and architects such as Theodore Link and Barnett, Haynes & Barnett.

On our bus tour, we also saw the other side of housing: the remains of high-rise public housing from the 1960s. Progressive urban planners, riding the wave of Lyndon Johnson's "war on poverty," designed large high-rise apartments for the poor which eventually became a nightmare for residents and politicians who trumpeted the solution to public housing. Residents were stacked like pancakes in poorly secured skyscrapers, and developments became a place to segregate large numbers of the poor.

These high-rises, like Pruitt-Igoe and Darst-Webbe in St. Louis, were eventually torn down and replaced by low-rise apartment developments that better mix low- and medium-income residents.

Toward the end of our tour, the bus took a turn onto Lake Shore Drive, the Forest Park Parkway-type roadway on the eastern edge of the neighborhood. But unlike St. Louis, Chicago has Lake Michigan, a visually stunning expanse of blue water and sailboats that we glimpsed from the top of our double-decker bus. The drive eventually turned into the Museum of Science Industry at the eastern edge of the UC campus.

Here things got *really* familiar. The museum is housed in the former Palace of Fine Arts, the only building existing from the 1893 World's Columbian Exposition, or known better as the Chicago World's Fair.

As we drove by the museum, I had a sense of *déjà vu*. Let's see… a World's Fair, a city park and an existing museum building. Sounds like the 1904 World's Fair and the Art Museum in Forest Park.

At the end of the tour, I talked to the guide, who was a UC administrator and professor in its urban planning department. I said I was from the St. Louis and the CWE, and he remarked on the similarities of our neighborhoods. He even said he had a good friend and colleague at — where else — Washington University.

While the CWE doesn't have a Barack Obama to claim, chances are he will sleep here someday — the Chase Hotel has hosted presidents and candidates over the years ranging from Harry Truman, John F. Kennedy and Richard Nixon.

A CARJACKING? DON'T BELIEVE EVERYTHING YOU READ

It was almost dusk, and I walked down the alley to my car.

It was parked in a deserted lot, and I hardly noticed the enveloping darkness as I fiddled with my keys.

I opened the door, sat down and started the car. I glanced into the rearview mirror and noticed there was a flyer stuck on my back window. It blocked my view, so I reluctantly climbed out of the car to grab it.

Suddenly, out of the corner of my eye, a figure darted from behind a nearby dumpster and lunged for my car door.

Before I could think, the figure jumped into my car, slammed the door and the car lurched into reverse.

I barely jumped out of the way, and my car sped off….

Don't believe everything you read.

The scenario above didn't happen; but according to an email I received last week, it's the latest carjacking scheme to terrorize St. Louis.

The email certainly seemed authentic. It was sent to me one busy morning by a relative, and I recognized several of the many people copied on the message.

The email quoted a Detective Bledsoe of the Florissant sheriff's office, and a Lt. Tony Bartholome of the Missouri Highway Patrol. These officials "confirmed" that this carjacking scheme had been used 13 times in August in the city and county, including three near the Fox Theatre.

Normally I don't forward messages like these, but the email seemed credible and I thought of people I could forward it to. I started a new email, with six forwardees, and I wrote a quick note; "Normally, I don't forward stuff like this, but it sounds legit."

But before I clicked "send," I paused. I read through the email again and noticed this phrase: "the Missouri Highway Patrol urges everyone to keep this email circulating — the more people who are aware of this the better."

It had the faint ring of the old chain letters I used to receive and I threw away.

At the end of the email was a phone number for the Missouri Neighborhood Association. On a whim, I called the number and it was no longer in service.

Curious, I grabbed a white-pages telephone book and looked up the Florissant sheriff's office. There wasn't a sheriff's number listed, so I called the non-emergency police number.

A woman's voice answered. "Yes, can I speak with Detective Bledsoe?" I asked.

A weary sigh came from the woman. "That email's a hoax. There is no Detective Bledsoe. That story's been around for 20 years."

Chagrined, I mumbled "sorry" and hung up.

My first reaction to this was to curse the advent of the internet and email. But like everything from the telephone to text messaging, email has become a ubiquitous form of modern communication. It's just a tool, and needs to be scrutinized — like sifting the bogus mortgage offers out of your daily "snail" mail.

Truth be told, like cell phones or fax machines, it's hard for me to imagine life before email and how I could manage my business and personal affairs without it.

Email provides a short-cut for many phone calls or meetings; it can also be an excuse *not* to call someone.

And when someone you know forwards you something that seems true, you're apt to believe it.

It reminds me of something that happened several years ago in my office. It was during the height of President Clinton's Monica Lewinsky scandal, and a college student working for us one summer stopped me as I walked by her computer.

"Uh, it says here on the Internet that the prosecutor has a list of books that Monica Lewinsky bought at the bookstore, and one was called *Telling Lies for Fun and Profit.*"

The college student looked at me and said. "Is that in the real news?"

I knew what she was thinking. Standing there, gray-haired and adult, I was the symbol of "real news," someone who read newspapers and watched serious TV news talk shows on Sunday mornings. I wanted to tell her: that's why you're in college, to learn to think critically about everything you read. But I just smiled, shook my head and went back to my office.

Ironically, the fake carjacking e-mail actually has a pretty good message. It's a reminder to city residents — and everyone these days — to be aware of your surroundings. True, it's unlikely a boogeyman will seize your car in such a manner, and the email breeds unwarranted fear, but it still has a point: You can never be too careful.

And don't believe everything you read.

TROUBLE RIGHT HERE IN RIVER CITY (2007)

Ya' got trouble, folks, *right here* in River City….

Somewhere in St. Louis, in a neighborhood filled with nice homes and apartments and condos, there's a place, which shall remain unnamed, where people bring their own bottles of beer and wine and who-knows-what, and they laugh and dance and sing and smoke well into the night.

On a *Thursday* night, no less.

No, this is not a wild Saturday night down on Laclede's Landing, Washington Avenue or the "east side" with big cars, flashy clothes, loud drunks and a hint of danger. No this is in a quiet little neighborhood — could be YOUR neighborhood — and these people are having entirely too much fun for a school night.

From the outside, the building is unremarkable, an old brick building, on a block with single-family homes. Out front there is a landmark, but I really can't say what it is. Let's just say it's big and colorful.

I'd heard about this place for a couple of years; many Thursday nights my oldest son would go and tell me about the live music and meeting his friends. On a recent Thursday, I was just sitting around the house, thinking about going to bed, when my son asked if I wanted to go. On a *Thursday* night? Why not?

I met him there around 9:15 p.m. When I entered the small building it was already packed with people and music was playing. I paid my $5 and adjusted my eyes to the dim light. I looked across the room and there was my son, waving to me from the front of the room at a small bar.

I squeezed by a bunch of young people dressed in black — excuse me! here comes the old guy! — and sat on an old permanent bar stool next to my son. "Sorry, Dad, that's the wobbly one, but at least we're close to the band."

Wobbly chair, indeed. But as I sat down, I realized it was the perfect place to absorb the atmosphere. As an amateur people-watcher and conversation-overhearer, this was a gold mine.

The main room is pretty small, maybe a half-dozen tables, the bar and some booths along one wall. There is even a rickety-looking balcony which was crammed with people. The walls were adorned with various kitschy pop-art items and a large D-I-N-E-R sign hung over the small stage. Everything was slightly shambled, like a one-star restaurant on a back alley in Paris. Dogs strolled around and people drank *straight from their wine bottle!* Trouble, indeed.

As I looked around I realized several things. One, I wasn't the oldest person there. In fact there were a couple of tables with couples my age sitting with young people, maybe their older kids. They seemed to be, in fact, *neighborhood* people who walked over after dinner. There were even people older than I — wearing berets and gray-haired ponytails — who had the smart-aleck smirks of "old hippies."

But the balance of the crowd was young people, early-twenty-somethings, in all kinds of garb. Some wore a lot of black, had stylish glasses and strategic facial hair. Others wore t-shirts and jeans, wild hair and jam-band t-shirts. And apparently "preppy" still lives — I met a nice young man with an argyle sweater, khakis and a "Hey, where'd you go to high school?" handshake.

Playing music was a well-known St. Louis blues band crowded on the stage next to the bar. The leader was a silky-voiced Smokey Robinson-styled singer who prowled through the crowd, letting people sing, and sometimes dancing with patrons. *Ain't too proud to beg…*

The place was a time warp. Was this the hideaway basement of a speakeasy in Prohibition-era St. Louis? A boozy literary bar in Paris? One of those "weekend only" clubs that open and close in vacant buildings, staying one step ahead of the city inspectors?

When the band took a break, my son led me on a tour. The owner, an artist, has created his own little world. From a creepy old wheelchair to a huge Bob's Big Boy-type figure in the side yard, this was clearly an alternate universe of retro furnishings and subversive décor.

When we got back to the bar, I saw the owner approach the stage and my son said, "Here he goes. You gotta listen to this."

Holding a box, the owner wished someone happy birthday in the crowd and then announced that the next day was *his* birthday. In honor of the occasion, he said, he was going to give away gifts.

"Here are some books my kids gave me for Christmas," he said. "I never read them, so I thought I'd give them away." His son and daughter, both of whom were working behind the bar, laughed knowingly. Good old Dad!

The owner then started to fling the books across the room — watch out! — to eager hands. Then he threw an old board game. Finally, he reached into the box and pulled out some, well, adolescent noise-creating gag devices, the kind that once upon a time I may have bought at Spicer's Five & Dime. He flung those, too, saying "be sure to use these in church, or in school."

The crowd — *his* crowd — went wild and clapped. Even a cynic would have to admit his irreverence was endearing, not in the least threatening.

After that we went upstairs with a friend of my son's, and we spent an hour talking politics and solving world problems in that earnest, passionate way I used to do in college.

Around 11 p.m., I realized I had to get home. I thanked my son, said goodbye to his friend and squeezed by a bunch of dancers who were moving to the band's second set. School night? Schmool night. The night was still young for them.

Before I left, my son had asked, "Dad, you're not going to write about this, are you?" How could I not? But apparently the place has gotten so popular that some neighbors have complained about the parking and the alley dumpsters getting too full. In fact, there were little postcards that said, "SEX! Now that I've got your attention, please carry home your own trash." Apparently word-of-mouth has made the place popular and the owner doesn't want or need the publicity. So I agreed not to name it.

So, trouble? I stepped into the cold night and thought: in a world of fern bars, chain restaurants and corporate logos, maybe this place *is* trouble.

That's trouble with a "T" that rhymes with "P" which means *perfect.* At least to cure the winter blahs on a Thursday night.

Update: the name of the establishment in the Skinker-DeBaliviere neighborhood was called "Christman's," for owner/artist Bill Christman, and it closed in 2008, due in part to neighborhood complaints. The landmark out front? A very large rooster.

DREAMING OF A 'GREEN' CHRISTMAS

It looks like we'll be having a "green" Christmas in my house this year. And I don't mean just the tree.

It actually started last summer when my second-oldest son, home from college, one day started picking through our kitchen trash.

"Dad, you're *killing* me," he said, exasperated, as he removed various pieces of plastic and cardboard I'd thrown away. My wife and other kids were away for the week, which meant there were a lot more disposable containers in the trash.

"Don't you read the numbers on the bottom of the plastic?" he asked.

No, actually I don't. Or didn't.

My son went away to college in Kirksville, Missouri. By the time he came home for summer the first year, he'd changed from an 18-year-old fast-food-eating high school graduate into a disciple of the "greening of America" movement. *Newsweek* said that environmentalism isn't just for Hollywood liberals and Prius-driving yuppies anymore. According to a Gallup poll, the number of Americans who say they worry about the environment "a great deal" or "a fair amount" increased from 62 to 77 percent between 2004 and 2006.

As *Newsweek* pointed out, the "new environmentalism" seems to be here to stay, from "sustainable" skyscrapers in Manhattan to waves of amber grain being turned into ethanol. Global warming, Katrina, Chinese industrialization… all are real-world issues that are seeping into the national consciousness.

My son's change at school included taking environmental classes and joining the biology department's "compost project." This involves students scraping uneaten food off of cafeteria trays and carting it to a farm near school. He became part of a bicycle-riding coop and involved in a group that encourages people not to use so many plastic bags.

I can relate in some way. When I was a kid in the 1970s, I remember the "ecology" movement. That was the time of the Clean Water Act, the EPA and acid rain. I remember being passionate about saving the environment; plus I had a cool bumper sticker on my school notebook with the "e" logo that looked a lot like a peace sign.

Now, we've become a more environmentally-aware family, thanks in part to my son but also to my wife, who has always abhorred waste. She washes cloth diapers for our baby, saves food for the compost pile and prowls the alleys for discarded treasures.

I'm guess I'm wired differently; there's something satisfying about throwing a huge bag of garbage into the dumpster. And it feels good trying to rid the house of the millions of cheap tiny plastic toys that sprout everywhere.

Cynics will say that a few people riding bikes to work instead of driving will do little to offset the 1.7 billion tons of carbon produced by U.S. vehicles. Or buying a "water efficient toilet" will only save a few gallons a year.

But it can add up, and I'm beginning to get into the spirit. I've gotten pretty good at sorting through paper and cardboard and I actually turn over the plastic cups and containers to see what recycling "number" they are.

I also walk to work when I can. It's only a few blocks and doesn't mean much in the big scheme of things, but it's good exercise. And sometimes I'll walk through an alley hoping to find a discarded chair or brass lamp I can drag home.

And the Christmas tree? An artificial tree might be more environmentally friendly, but we always get a real tree. When it's time, I'll bring it to Forest Park to be ground up into pine mulch. I guess I could carry it a block or two to the park, but I think I'll drive.

RED LIGHT RUNNERS AND CAMERAS

There's a saying, "all politics is personal."

I was reminded of this last week. I heard that the city of St. Louis was considering installing cameras at intersections to keep track of people who run red lights.

How is it personal? Five years ago one morning, I stood at the corner of Lindell and Kingshighway boulevards, picking shards of a car glass window out of my four-year-old son's hair.

We'd just been involved in a traffic accident. Right before the collision, I'd sat poised in my car at the intersection, anxious to make it to my son's school on time.

When the light turned green, my car the first one at the intersection, I glided into the street.

Unbeknownst to me, because a truck next to me was blocking my sight, the driver of a Honda S.U.V. traveling west on Lindell had run the red light at Kingshighway. As I sped through the intersection, in a blur I noticed the Honda coming at me. In a split second, the Honda smashed into the back end of my car, just a foot or two away from my son in the back seat. My car spun around several times, and I saw the Honda roll a couple times through the intersection.

Thankfully, no one in my car was hurt. The Honda driver? I don't know, but the car was still upside down when the paramedics got to it.

One thing I learned from the accident was to be extremely patient when waiting at red lights, especially in the city. Even if the light turns green, now I will wait a few seconds — the time it takes a car behind me to honk — to make sure there aren't any speeders coming through the intersection.

Ironically, before the accident, I had started a mini-campaign against red-light-runners in my own neighborhood. There is a stoplight near my house which I pass through every morning taking kids to school or going to work. Alarmed at the number of cars speeding through, I started taking down license plate numbers, times and car descriptions. I wasn't sure what I'd do with the list, but after a couple of months, I sent it to the police department and talked to a captain. He said he couldn't do anything with the list, but he said it did show evidence of a problem and he promised to beef up patrols. For a while, at least, there were more police cars around.

So, what about cameras? The city of Arnold recently installed three cameras, the first city in Missouri to do so. The devices will photograph the license plates of cars running through red lights, and car owners will get tickets by mail. Drivers will not be photographed.

Such cameras are used in about 20 states. How do they work? Generally, a sensor in the pavement signals a camera to take a picture of a vehicle that enters an intersection after the traffic light turns red. The camera records a second image showing the car, its license number and driver. Some systems use a second camera to get a head-on picture of the driver. The company that operates the system sends the photos to police, who review the evidence and forward to prosecutors cases deemed to show clear violations.

Of course, there are those who object to the cameras, citing privacy and "Big Brother is watching" concerns. There's also a question whether such camera photographs can be considered legal evidence . The ticket is sent to the owner of the vehicle, but what if someone else is driving? What if the picture reveals people in the car that the owner really doesn't want others to know are in the car (if you catch my drift)?

According to a recent article in the *St. Louis Post-Dispatch*, results are mixed on whether the cameras really increase traffic safety. One report cited a jump in rear-end collisions at intersections with cameras. This was caused apparently by people changing their mind at the last second to stop at a light. But studies in both Phoenix and Ontario, Canada, showed that cameras reduced injury accidents by up to 11 per cent. And the Insurance Institute for Highway Safety has said 22 per cent of all traffic accidents in the United States are caused by drivers running red lights. About 800 people die each year in such crashes, which cause an estimated $7 billion in property damage, medical bills, lost productivity and insurance hikes, the institute said.

There's also a cost issue. The camera program in Phoenix requires a $400,000 annual subsidy. But in Arnold, it's not costing the city a dime; the camera company takes a $31 dollar cut out of the $94.50 fine that's collected.

So, if I were king, I'd put cameras at every major intersection in the city. Privacy? Schmivacy. If you're running red lights, I think everyone should know.

And I take it personally.

DID YOU GIVE TO YOUR LOCAL PANHANDLER?

The season for giving has just passed. Did you give to your local panhandler?

In 1981, when I was a senior at St. Louis University, I was walking back to my dorm (Lewis Hall, now the Coronado apartments) after my final first-semester exam. I was in a great mood; I was done with school, heading home that afternoon and had a date that night. As I approached the dorm, a man approached me for money. I stopped, pulled out my wallet and gave him a dollar bill. Later, in my dorm room, I checked my wallet and realized I had given him a *$20* bill instead of a $1 bill. I felt cheated, but I wasn't sure why. As a liberal college student, I certainly believed in giving to those in need. But $20? That was my date money.

About a month ago, I was standing at the corner of Forsyth Boulevard and Meramec Avenue in downtown Clayton. I was leaving a meeting, and was dressed in my "Clayton clothes" (a tie and sports coat). Out of the corner of my eye, I saw a man approaching, and he asked if I had any spare change. I politely declined, as I usually do, and I realized that here, among the corporate towers and cell phones, I never expected to be approached.

I have mixed feelings about panhandlers. On the one hand, the encounter can be annoying and even uncomfortable. On the other, I've come to accept it as part of the fabric of urban living. As long as I'm not verbally abused or feel threatened physically, I don't believe undue police action should be used to remove them. But then again, I don't own a shop or restaurant where panhandlers can discourage customers.

Generally my policy is to politely refuse. Sometimes I say, "Sorry, I don't have anything," and that's because I rarely have any cash on hand. I know one long-time city resident who carries a book of McDonald's gift certificates to give to panhandlers.

My polite-refusal policy can backfire, though. I once "profiled" a man approaching me as I walked home from work in the Central West End and before he could speak, I shook my head as if to refuse him. He looked at me and said he needed directions.

And there's the irony of walking out of church, being approached by a panhandler, refusing to give money and then reflecting on the "when I was poor…" part of Christianity. Was that a panhandler or was it Jesus? That's hard for me to reconcile no matter what I think the panhandler would do with the money I would give him.

Ultimately, I rationalize my polite refusal as an issue of personal safety. One day as I walked the three blocks to work, a panhandler approached me. As I normally do, I did not meet his eyes and mumbled, "Sorry I can't help you." Instead of moving on, this man challenged me. For some reason, I took the bait. I started arguing with him, telling him that I don't carry any cash. He laughed as if he didn't believe me, and then I took out my wallet and started to show him… and then I realized how dangerous that might be. When I was in college, I had a lot less to lose. Being responsible for a family now, I don't want to take any risks.

Another time, I was raking leaves in my front yard when a man approached me. When I looked up, he immediately put up his hands and said, "Don't worry! I'm not one of the bad people."

I'm sure you're not, I thought as I politely refused him.

I just don't want to take the chance.

SCENE OF THE CRIME: MY GARAGE

The young woman police officer stood in the front hall of my house, seeming bored and distracted. I couldn't blame her; it was a hot and humid Thursday night and I'm sure the reason I called 911 was the least of her concerns that night.

Earlier that evening, my wife had told me that it looked like the metal grate over one of the windows of our garage had been kicked in. This had happened a couple of years before; someone pushed in the grate, got into our garage and taken a lawn mower and a couple of bikes. We hadn't called the police then, partly because we had no idea when it happened and partly because, well, I didn't want to "bother" the police over a minor burglary.

I went out to the garage, and like a bad *CSI* television actor, "surveyed the scene." It didn't take Sherlock Holmes to figure out what happened. The metal grates over the windows were not very secure; I had nailed them in and sometimes even a strong soccer ball kick would knock them into the garage. When I peered into the garage, it looked like the overhead door was still closed and nothing was taken. Truth was, the perpetrator probably looked in and decided it wasn't worth the effort to climb in and take some old wood, a plastic outdoor pool, a shovel with a broken handle, or a wheelbarrow with flat tires. Since our previous break-in, I had tried not to put anything too valuable in the garage. You want that plastic trash can with a lid chewed up by squirrels? Go ahead.

I walked over to the garage's entry door and saw that the padlock had been jammed and the latch was bent. I looked down and there was a broken broom broken which we had left on our porch. Apparently, the would-be burglar tried to break into the door, then pushed in the window before fleeing empty-handed.

I went back into the house and called 911 without hesitation. I think I wanted to somehow make up for the last time this happened and didn't call the police. Also, there had been several other garage break-ins on our street recently – some a lot more serious than mine – and I wanted to make sure there was a record of my incident.

As I waited on hold for 911, I wondered what real emergencies were out there in the summer night. Did I really want to bother the city's finest with a botched burglary?

But I remembered what the neighborhood security people and the police always said at meetings: make the call. It was one of the unwritten rules of city living. The more police calls you make, the more attention you get.

I also thought that while property values have soared since we moved to the Central West End in 1992, and crime rates generally have dropped, it still can be a dangerous city. People who are paying a lot more than I did for their home or condo are moving into the neighborhood thinking it's Webster Groves East. Yes, it's a great, vibrant area, but you need to have street smarts and be "aware of your surroundings." Yes, crime can happen anywhere, but our neighborhood consists of relatively affluent people living in close proximity to people who aren't, and statistically we're more at risk.

When the 911 operator came on the line, I immediately told her that my complaint was "minor" and I just wanted to make a phone report about the attempted burglary. The operator said they were required to send out an officer.

As I waited I went back outside and remembered that the gate on our side yard was unlocked. A contractor had to get access to the back yard the day before, so I had unlocked the gate and had forgotten to replace it. Whether the burglar had gone through the side gate or not, it was on open door to our backyard. Knowing that most incidents like these are "crimes of opportunity" and sometimes the smallest obstacles will thwart a thief, it was really careless on my part to leave the gate unlocked.

I also looked around the back yard and realized how dark it was. We have a spotlight on the porch, but it barely illuminates the garage. I resolved to call to get prices on putting in more lights. I noticed the garage window again and I knew I had to secure the gates better. Then I almost laughed when I saw the small chicken coop in the far corner of the yard. Our hens are good for providing eggs, but apparently not Vicious Guard Chickens when it comes to backyard intruders.

When the police officer came, she wrote down the information and gave me a card with the case number on it. I told her that I was sorry she had to come out on such a relatively minor matter, and she said it was a policy to respond to all calls. And like a confessor at church, I admitted I'd been careless about leaving the side gate unlocked and the grates unsecured. She just shrugged.

Her police radio suddenly cackled about who-knows-what-else was brewing out on the streets that night. She left and while I was glad I "made the call" I knew a little more vigilance on my part would have saved us all some trouble.

WILY COYOTES IN FOREST PARK?

If you read the *St. Louis Post-Dispatch* recently, you learned that there are "killer coyotes" in Ladue. These are wild animals that are attacking residents' pets (not humans) thanks to that ever-growing suburban problem of humans "encroaching" on animal territory. A similar issue, you'll recall, is the deer infestation of Town & Country and Creve Coeur.

Here in the city, our major "infestation" problems are the more traditional squirrels, possums and — when someone renovates their house on your street — mice. But when I read the *Post* story, I realized that we might have our own coyote neighbors.

(As an aside, I think the *Post* handled the story in a very fair-minded manner. However, part of me wishes the old tabloid *St. Louis Sun* newspaper was still around, the newspaper that once blared a big headline about some unfortunate victim being "sawed in half." How would they have treated the coyote story? Make up your own tabloid headline here.)

Some months ago, my 15-year-old son announced that he'd seen a coyote in Forest Park. He saw the animal one morning on the way to school at C.B.C. high school. My older son, who's 18, drives him to school each day.

I didn't really believe him at first. You have to consider the circumstances. Exactly how observant is a drowsy teenager at seven in the morning as his brother speeds down on off-ramp with Phish music blaring? And this from a kid who's well-meaning but once spent part of a day looking for his shoes that he didn't notice he was wearing. Still, when I questioned him further about the sighting, he was quite sure that it wasn't just a stray dog.

About a week before Christmas, I went jogging in Forest Park. I got started later than I wanted, and found myself in near-dark about halfway through the park. Getting tired, I decided to take a short-cut and I started down the path that runs behind the Art Museum.

Or should I say, that *used* to run behind the Art Museum.

You would need a daily press briefing to keep up with all of the construction changes in the park as we near the 2004 deadline for park improvements. I was unaware that they had torn up the path behind the museum. The path got muddier as I ran, and, ignoring orange construction netting, I kept jogging as the path turned to gravel and then to no path at all. I stopped on a hill, my shoes covered with mud, and I looked to find the best way to navigate my way back.

Even though I was in the middle of a big city, there was something quite peaceful about standing in the park after a winter sunset, with silver streaks of gray in the sky, and an unusual quiet.

My little Thoreau moment was suddenly interrupted by some movement in the brush ahead of me. Uh-oh, I thought, so much for "street smarts." I was alone in the park, in the dark, at the edge of Kennedy Forest and a quarter mile from the museum.

Suddenly, a four-legged creature trotted out of the brush about twenty feet in front of me. Even in the dim light it was clear this wasn't a dog. It had a sleek silver coat, a long pointed face and moved with the grace of a wild animal unaccustomed to restraint. I froze and held my breath. The animal — a wily coyote? — paid me absolutely no mind and glided effortlessly across the field and into the woods.

It turns out my son was right. I checked with Anabeth Calkins, executive director of Forest Park, and she knows of at least two coyotes in the park. Other wildlife that has been spotted include red foxes, great horned owls and even a deer, she said.

According to the *Post* story, coyotes normally feed on rodents… like squirrels and possums. Maybe the coyote I saw should tell his friends in Ladue to forget the pets and move to Forest Park. We have plenty of possums here.

RUNNING ON EMPTY (1998)

6:05 a.m. I jog into Forest Park at Lindell and Union boulevards, dodging hell-bent commuters until I find the darkened bike path. I head west, past Cabanne House. It's a cool, late March morning and already I'm regretting my decision to start yet another fitness regime.

6:12 a.m. This is my favorite stretch of the run — it's flat. As I pass, I glance at the homes on Lindell Boulevard, classic Tudors alternating with white moderns and even one with porthole windows.

6:15 a.m. I pass the History Museum, large cranes lurking behind the main building. I think about the twin 30-foot diameter sewers under my feet, sewers built to contain the Des Peres river before the 1904 World's Fair.

6:18 a.m. At Des Peres Road I look over at the large mansion built by Mike Faille, who owned Talayna's restaurant. Though it's been finished for a year, it still looks out of scale, even with the other mansions on the street. Some trees would help.

6:18 a.m. I near the western end of the park and in the corner of my eye I see the Art Museum, sitting atop the Mount Everest that is Art (Heartbreak) Hill. I feel like turning back... but then I always feel like turning back. To my left I see geese swimming in new ponds created by the latest rainfall; to my right I see more park space reclaimed by construction equipment.

6:20 a.m. Golfers will always be with us in Forest Park, no matter the time of day, time of year or weather. I see one, scooting the ball along the wet fairway grass, cursing as he goes. This is fun?

6:26 a.m. There's no denying it... Art Hill calls. I start wheezing, plodding one step at a time. At the top, through sweat and between gasps, I see a colorful sunrise light up the vista to the north towards DeBaliviere Avenue and the radio tower. I imagine what park planners say will be an open space in the center of the park without cris-crossing roads. I also imagine being back home, in bed.

6:28 a.m. Up ahead I see shapes and hear spirited laughter. The ground rumbles and in a blur of brightly-colored lycra, a group of 20 runners bounds past me. Must be the 6:20 club. One yells out to me entirely too cheerfully, "Good morning, runner!" Try decaf, buddy.

6:35 a.m. I pass one of the park's most dangerous crossings — where Hampton Avenue enters the park. Cut-through drivers barely pause before turning right on a red light. Fix that, master planners!

6:40 a.m. I turn north and pass the Jewel Box. Behind it are two forgotten monuments, one to the Korean War dead, the other a set of gates to the once-grand, now-demolished Vandeventer Place.

6:45 a.m. Past the newly renovated Muny, a man stands placidly by himself at the shore of a lake holding a remote control device. He's directing a loud, miniature speedboat across the water. Whatever floats your boat.

6:50 a.m. I leave the park via Union Boulevard. I pass New City School, its "urban campus" impressive, and turn for home. I think ahead to the work day.

I'll limp and groan, but I'll remember the sunrise.

CHICKEN JOURNAL:

A CHICKEN CONDO

The condo-building craze in the Central West End has reached my own back yard.

Construction was slowed by wet weather and by the fact that the contractor had a lot of other commitments. But the occupants recently moved into a new A-frame loft.

I don't mean to be cagey, but because of city ordinances and neighbors, let's just say it's a group home for "several" single females. I don't charge much for rent — just a few eggs a day.

Yes, our chickens have a new home.

Regular readers of this column might know that three years ago my wife and kids decided to start "keeping" chickens. I was skeptical at first — with all of our kids, we have enough living things to feed. But how can you refuse a wide-eyed eight year old? My wife did a lot of research on the "urban chicken movement" (there's a club for everything) and one morning came home from Soulard market with five chicks.

Those five eventually became four when one turned out to be a rooster. Those became three this past January when one of the chickens died which was sad for the family, but it was also a good way to explain to the kids the "cycle of life."

Naturally, we thought of getting more chickens (well, actually, they did). Why not? Overall the experience has been good. But it was time for them to have a new home.

Their original quarters consisted of various wooden boxes my son and I cobbled together with a lot of nails and duct tape. And — my wife is proud to say — all of the crates came from discards in the alley.

Basically, the set-up consisted of three boxes, one bigger than the next. The smallest was the "nesting box," a small area where the hens could have a little privacy and lay eggs. The "coop" was the covered living area which had food and water and a perch for sleeping at night. Then there was a larger "run," basically a big square mesh cage where the birds would spend the day. This is necessary in the city, where various predators like possums might decide to have chicken for lunch.

The biggest issue with chicken-keeping is how one manages the "waste." We had devised a system where every month or so, we'd moved the entire coop to another spot in the backyard. Because of the chicken-made fertilizer, I'd hoe up the ground, throw down some grass seed, and the old spot would soon sprout new grass.

But after three years, this moving around took its toll on the coop. It was time to build something new.

Though I hadn't seen it, my son described another coop he'd seen in a city back yard. It was an A-frame construction, with separate levels for the perch and for the food. It also had a removable floor; the idea was that this would catch the waste and one could clean it off.

One Saturday in late March, the day dawned free of commitments. I sat down and tried to sketch out exactly how we would build it, but after a while, I just grabbed one of my sons and we went to Home Depot. We felt that primeval male urge to Build Something.

I don't have a glorious background in construction. I can hammer nails and use a jig saw, but most of my experience consisted of putting together shelves or a pinewood derby car for Cub Scouts. My son, however, owned a real tool belt and had used power tools at school.

By the end of that Saturday we had finished the frame for the coop. Improvising along the way, we had come up with a design that would combine into one structure the nesting box, the coop and the run.

I figured one more day and we'd have the thing done. But March turned into April, which turned into May, and the wooden triangle frame sat unfinished in the back yard. We needed a deadline, and that came in late May with the impending graduation party for my daughter.

As any homeowner knows, having a party causes a lot of things to be done around the house. Painting, gardening, garage-cleaning, etc., all seem to get done in the days before having an event at your house. So it was with the coop.

Finishing it was a lot harder than starting it. Now I realize why architects have detailed plans *before* they start building. Though I tried to think through various parts of the construction, we'd get to a certain point and just, well, hammer in a lot of nails and cut more wood to "make it fit." We spent just about every evening after dinner until it was dark in the frenzied last few days before the party to finish the coop.

But it worked out fine. The coop has a removable floor and a loft for the perch. We ended up using two parts of the old coop to make it big enough for all of the chickens.

As for the new tenants, they seem to like it and so far there have been no complaints — although now that their quarters have been upgraded, I wouldn't mind a few more eggs.

SECTION VII

Dad, You're Right (College and Young Adult)

CAN I PLEASE GO BACK TO COLLEGE?

Can I go back to school?

Please?

I never used to feel this way, but in the span of about a month, I will have visited four different college campuses, a high school and a grade school. I have children in five schools this fall, and for the first time, as I near my 30th high school reunion, I'm actually nostalgic about school.

When I graduated from college, I was ready to enter the work force. Armed with a solid liberal arts degree, I just figured I would throw myself into the world and deal with it. Luckily, I was saved from attending law school (my "other option") when I got a Real Job, and I never looked back. I knew many people who went on in school for advanced degrees, or night school, but I couldn't stand the thought of sitting still again in another classroom. I never "got" people who said they missed school and would be full-time students again if they had the chance.

Now I think I get it.

My first back-to-school moment was in late August when I drove my second-oldest son and his futon to Kirksville. He's a junior and was moving into a house with three other people.

We borrowed a truck, but other than a futon, his stuff was basically a pile of clothes, his camping gear, an end table, his stereo and his banjo. Within a half hour of getting to his house, his room was done. We walked a couple of blocks toward campus and strolled through the tree-lined walkways among the big old buildings. Kids were all around, walking or riding bikes, and the air was fresh from the nearby farms and countryside.

I tried to remember when I had so few possessions, so few things to do except to set up house and get ready for school.

And what was school, anyway? Just reading books and going to classes? I could do that again.

Last week, I was on the campus of University of Missouri-St. Louis, which my oldest son attends. I wasn't there for back-to-school activities, but I hadn't been on the campus in a long time.

I was amazed at how much UMSL looks like a "real" campus; in my experience, it was primarily a commuter state school. A good school, yes, but more utilitarian than the traditional college-school-brochure institution with ivy-covered walls.

But I was pleasantly surprised when I visited radio station KWMU. The school *had* become a campus, with green walkways, ponds and shiny new glass buildings. I walked through the student center and there were fresh-faced kids with laptops and bookbags, and I marveled at the size of the cafeteria and the wide selection of food.

Wouldn't it be nice if all you had to do to eat, at any time of day, was to just pick what food you'd like, swipe your student card and go?

My niece is a freshman at St. Louis University, my alma mater, and we had a chance to visit her in her dormitory, Griesedieck Hall, the high-rise building in the center of campus.

While I am familiar with the campus, the last time I'd set foot in that dorm was in 1981.

From the 11th floor of her dorm room, my niece has a great view of the city looking south. Looking at her loft bed, iPod stereo and mini-refrigerator, I remembered again how relatively simple college life is. You can dash over to the recreation center, cafeteria, library or class in a matter of minutes, with no thought of cars or highway construction.

My third oldest son attends high school, and at his "back to school" night, along with hundreds of other parents, I walked through all of his classes and met his teachers in a simulation of his school day.

The teachers all seemed pleasant, witty and eager to teach our children. I thought about high school and the certainty of the class schedule, day after day: the relief at three o'clock, the camaraderie of sports teams and the biggest concern being getting a ride to the weekend dance or football game.

But then there was chemistry… and I remembered the "dark side" of high school, for myself, being anything related to math or science. My son's chemistry teacher was nice enough, but I'd walked in late and sat in the front row. I had to spend the next 15 minutes staring at a huge poster of the periodic elements and recalling Bunsen-burners, beakers and Boron. I have to say that I really don't use a single thing today I learned in high school chemistry, although I still remember what a "meniscus" is.

I take our younger kids to their grade school most mornings, and on "back to school" day, two of my three said they "couldn't wait" for school to start. I walked the school's shining tile floors and past fresh-scrubbed walls, everything bright and cheery with welcoming posters and smiling teachers. I remembered my own parents asking me what the best part of our day was, like we ask our kids, and the answers were similar: lunch, recess and snack time. In grade school, the rules were simple: wear your uniform, don't butt in line, find a partner, clean up your mess, check your homework, be on time.

Next weekend, we drive our oldest daughter and her shoes to start college in Chicago. We'd visited the campus last March, and it truly is one of those "ivy-covered wall" places. While my Kirksville son's main concern was making sure his old record turntable worked, my daughter wanted to make sure her dorm room bedspread matches the "color scheme" of her room. But that's OK, because soon she'll be able to get to explore a big city that I'd love to know better, one with tremendous museums and neighborhoods, views of the lake and many skyscrapers. If it wasn't for the Cubs, I'd probably also want to live there.

I've never attended a high school reunion, but with my newfound school appreciation, I decided I'd attend my 30th this year. Then I checked the date and realized it's the same weekend we take our daughter to Chicago.

High school will have to wait.

COLLECT CALL FROM FRANCE

I got a call earlier this week from one of my kids. He was worried because his ride hadn't shown up yet.

When you have kids, this is not an unusual call. Keeping track of who's going where and when, and how they're getting home is always a juggling act.

But this call was different. It was a collect call at four in the morning. It was from my oldest son, who was phoning from a train station in Paris. My sister was supposed to meet him there after his all-night flight from Boston, but he couldn't find her. Apparently, they hadn't agreed on a place to meet and the Gare du Nord train station was as cavernous as Grand Central Station. Our son was tired from flying all night and alone in a strange country where he didn't know the language.

This was our first child to go abroad. After meticulous planning, here he was, just hours after we said goodbye, asking us to help with a problem 3,000 miles away. My wife found it ironic that while our eight-week old baby slept soundly through the night, it was our 20 year old kid that was keeping us up at four a.m.

Our son's immediate plight was complicated by the fact that he didn't speak French and he didn't have a cell phone. He was calling from a pay phone. As my wife tried to calm him down, I got on my cell phone and called my sister, who was wandering around the other side of the huge train depot.

They eventually met, we hung up and tried to go back to sleep. Later, it seemed like a surreal dream.

People younger than I may not think international phone-calling is a big deal, but I do. To be able to talk to my son like he was in the same room, but half a world away, still amazes me. This is not an anti-cell phone rant, but one of the problems with the technology is that we now expect to be able to talk to anyone, anywhere in the world, instantly.

It made me think of a time 25 years ago when my future wife was studying in France. Most of our communication was "par avion," or air mail, and I would anxiously await the mail each day.

In the course of her six-month stay, I talked to her on the phone maybe two or three times, and those were big events. She was living in an old convent, with just one phone for the whole building, and we'd plan ahead for weeks for a phone call. We'd set a certain time, usually early in the morning for me, and I'd go through the operator to place the call. I'd hear all kinds of switches and clicks and beeps and try to imagine the phone call going underneath the Atlantic Ocean through the transatlantic cable. Sometimes the call went through, sometimes not; it was always a miracle when I heard her voice on the other end.

Now, you hit a button on your cell phone, the signals bounce off of a satellite and land on a phone thousands of miles away and you can chat away like you were across town.

My son's visit to Paris was just a brief stopping point. His final destination is Greece, where he will take an archaeological course through his school, U.M.-St. Louis. It's a great opportunity, and he earned a partial scholarship, but our expense budget didn't include transatlantic collect calls because he couldn't find his ride.

But since that first day, we've been getting regular e-mails from him and he seems to have gotten the hang of foreign travel after his first rocky experience.

Still, if the phone rings and it's the middle of the night, and the operator asks… "would you accept a collect call…" I might be tempted to say, "No, but can you tell my son to just get a cab?"

WHY AREN'T THESE KIDS IN THE LIBRARY?

So, this is college life.

It was very early on a Friday morning as I walked back to the hotel with my 17-year-old son. We had just left a concert in Columbia, Missouri, at the Blue Note, a small downtown music club. For the preceding three hours, I had been with him and his older brother at a Yonder Mountain String Band concert.

For the first half of the show I stood next to my sons in the front row of the club, shoulder to shoulder with hundreds of college kids as they danced to the bluegrass music. As I looked around at the crowd, I kept thinking: it's a school night, shouldn't they be at the library? Dating myself further, I also thought: it's 11 o'clock... do their parents know where they are? (The kids around me were probably thinking: who IS this old guy?)

It was actually my idea to go to the concert to see my son's favorite band as a way to combine a birthday present with a college visit. We weren't there to visit the University of Missouri at Columbia (Mizzou), but it was a half-way point to our primary destination, Truman State University in Kirksville, Missouri.

We three had done the Mizzou visit a year ago, when my oldest son was thinking about going there. He later decided to attend the University of Missouri at St. Louis. Part of his reasoning, he said, was that he felt he'd have "too much fun" at Mizzou and it would be a waste of money. This surprisingly mature statement coming out of his mouth – judging by the concert we attended — was probably true.

I don't mean to be unfair to Mizzou, but the concert did illustrate the temptations — I mean "social opportunities" — a large state school in a medium-sized town can offer. Mizzou is a great school, but you have to have the self-discipline and motivation to stay on track. If you're prone to "having fun," you may end up back home if you don't pull at least a 2.0 grade point average.

The next morning we went up to Kirksville, a pleasant hour-and-a-half drive from Columbia. I had heard a lot about the school. It had a national reputation as a "good college value" and it was known for drawing kids from the upper end academically of their high school classes. I also heard it was in a small town in northern Missouri — too small to have a club like the Blue Note, I thought.

I was wrong about one thing: it's not just a small town. It's in the middle of nowhere. I've never been to North Dakota, but Kirksville must be similar. I don't mean to sound like a city snob, but compared to Kirksville, Columbia seemed like New York City.

But being in a small town doesn't necessarily ensure your kid will go to the library. In fact, a couple of years ago, a friend said that within a few days of dropping his son off at Truman to start school, he got a call saying that his son had been in a fight with some Kirksville "townies" at a local bar. Temptation can lurk anywhere, even in North Dakota.

Overall, I was extremely impressed with Truman. It has a relatively small campus that is concentrated in a single area. Many of the dormitories are right in the middle of campus, and even the "off campus" housing is adjacent to the school. The buildings are a pleasing mix of historic architecture and modern, airy, brightly-lit structures.

And while it is relatively small (5700 students vs. 35,000 at Mizzou), it's not too tiny. The school has a strong liberal arts curriculum with 45 majors available. At any one time, about 500 students are studying at programs overseas, from England to Australia. Most first-year classes are taught by professors, not graduate students, and average class size is 27. At Mizzou, most freshman will experience at least one large class in a lecture hall with 100 students or more.

And while it's in a very small town, it has a mix of city and rural kids. Fully one-third of the students are from the St. Louis area. Another chunk are from Kansas City. An admissions counselor told me there are over 200 student activities and clubs, implying that you can find enough to do on campus.

One of the best aspects? The price of tuition. For a full academic year, the cost is less than $10,000, including room and board. And that's before any scholarships or financial aid.

Ten thousand dollars seems like a lot of money and it is, but if you've been shopping colleges recently, it's a bargain. Private college tuition can range from $25,000 to $40,000 a year.

That's a main reason why a lot of parents are re-examining state schools. When I was in college, state schools were only a couple of thousand dollars a year at most, and private schools were more, but not the cost of one fully loaded S.U.V. per year, like they are today.

While state school tuitions have soared in recent years because of state budget crunches (and mismanagement, but that's another story), it's still possible to get a comparable education for at least one-half the cost of a private school.

In my day, since state schools were relatively cheap, they generally drew more students that either couldn't academically qualify for a private school or couldn't afford it.

But the fact is, because of their tremendous resources, state schools have always provided a great education. And, as other parents remind me, unless you go to an Ivy League school, or you want to go to a top professional school, it really doesn't matter from which school you graduate. For most jobs (or graduate schools), success depends on how well you're prepared and how hard you work. After a while, no one cares or asks where you got your degree.

As the admissions person at Truman said, we're lucky to be in a state with a number of good public universities. It depends on the personality of your own kid, what he or she likes and needs to do well.

For all I know, half the kids at the concert may have studied all afternoon and not had classes the next day until 10 a.m.

And the other half might have been kids who drove down from Truman.

HOW TO AVOID THE 'EMPTY NEST'

I figured out one way to avoid the "empty nest" syndrome.

Just have a lot of kids.

This occurred to me last weekend when I was driving on Highway 63 near Moberly, Missouri, after taking my second oldest son to his first year of college. He is attending Truman State University, an oasis of liberal arts education in the cornfields of northern Missouri.

With me was my oldest daughter, a junior in high school. Meanwhile, at home, five younger kids were rapidly plotting how they would take over the space recently vacated by my college-bound son as well as his older brother, a UM-St. Louis student who'd just moved out of our house into a nearby carriage house.

In the space of a month, we moved our oldest two kids out of the house, leaving six to fight over the spoils. Among the six, however, was a new kid born on April Fool's day. So I've been telling people, we have a net loss of only one kid. (Although my sister pointed out that really, replacing two large boys with a tiny one is a net *gain*: our food and gas bills would shrink noticeably. She also warned me that they may come back again… as "boomerang" kids.)

We'd spent a hectic morning moving our son into the dormitory, hauling boxes, setting up computers, checking out food plans and bookstore options. But as I drove home along Highway 63, a.k.a."Pearl Harbor Memorial Highway" (why is it called that?), I thought about a speech that Truman's vice president of student affairs Dr. Lou Ann Gilchrist gave the incoming freshmen and their parents that morning.

She said that "launching" a child into adulthood was just a part of successful child rearing. Whether they move out of the house or go to college, at some point you have to let go and hope that your years of quiet and not-so-quiet direction will sink in. Most kids adopt the values of their parents, she said, and eventually you want to become less a disciplinarian and more a mentor.

Gilchrist described her own experience the day she moved her oldest child into college. As a mother, she felt compelled to make her son's dorm room bed, knowing full well that a teenage boy on his own would never think of that. It was her last attempt to exert motherly influence over her son. Her son rolled his eyes and kept quiet. But then when she started putting his socks and underwear into his dresser drawer in front of his new roommate, her son finally spoke up and made it clear he could finish unpacking.

I thought again about the kids at home and the busy week ahead.

School was starting for my two daughters and my three younger boys were entering their second week. There was painting and furniture-moving we still had to do to put kids into the third floor space vacated by their older brothers. And I realized we would for the first time in many years have a "spare" room for my wife and I to use as a guest room (or as a quiet escape). It was finally happening; more space for ourselves.

With the kids remaining at home, it would be another decade or so before we had a truly empty nest. I'd done the math; I'd been a young parent, and I would be an old parent. I clung to the notion that "children keep you young." With eight kids aged zero to twenty, we'd clearly embraced that strategy.

As the car neared Columbia, I flashed back to that morning when we were in my son's dorm room. We watched as he tried to cram his worldly belongings into the small room he was sharing with two other boys.

My daughter (under instruction from my wife) dutifully climbed up the bunk-bed ladder and carefully made his bed.

But I let him unpack his *own* socks and underwear. After all, you have to grow up sometime.

GOING TO KANSAS CITY

Until a recent weekend, I had never visited Kansas City.

Granted, I'd gone *through* the town many times on the way and back from Denver, but I'd never had a reason to stop.

My only view of the city was from my windshield as I sped down I-70. There was the Royals baseball stadium, scene of the 1985 meltdown by the Cardinals in the World Series — not exactly a pleasant sight. Or the bland suburban exits of Blue Springs and the non descript skyscrapers of downtown.

Then there was the "St. Louis snob" attitude I carried; in my mind, Kansas City was a "cowtown" that touted its barbecue and, well, its barbecue. But everything else compared poorly to St. Louis. Jazz and popular music? Sorry, we had Scott Joplin before he left for Sedalia, not to mention Miles Davis (okay, *East* St. Louis), Gaslight Square, Tina Turner and, well, Nelly. Baseball? Yes we lost in 1985, but the Royals have lost 100 games four of the last five years while the Cardinals have won more games than any other National League team since 2000. Literature? We can claim Tennessee Williams, T.S. Eliot and William Burroughs. The only writer I can think of from Kansas City is Calvin Trillin, who writes for the *New Yorker.* History? St. Louis was a proud French town founded before there was a United States, while K.C. is named for another state.

And I don't even *like* barbecue.

We visited K.C. because our oldest daughter, a senior in high school, had been invited to compete for a scholarship at Rockhurst University. Parents were invited, and it seemed like a good excuse to escape the St. Louis winter blahs for awhile.

This was the second "college visit" I'd had with my daughter. About a year ago, we'd gone to Chicago to see a couple of schools. And we're probably not done; unlike her older brothers, who both applied and were accepted to state schools, my daughter has applied to six colleges, most of them private. This reminds me that women *are* from Venus and men — like myself and my sons — are from Mars.

My daughter is from planet "I Care About School." Don't get me wrong — I'm extremely proud of her. But after having to bribe one of my sons to get out of bed in March of his senior year of high school to take the ACT so that he could go to *some* college, my daughter comes from another world.

She has a high G.P.A. at her high school, she's taking four college-level courses and — gasp! — she's still concerned about her studies in the second semester of her senior year.

Contrast that to my planet, where I knew exactly where I was going to college because my Dad taught there. I slouched through the SAT and worked only hard enough in college to finish in four years and keep a solid "B" average. My biggest ambition was to finish school so that I could go to work.

So when Rockhurst offered this opportunity, we figured we'd make a weekend of it. And I could finally decide if K.C. is a real town, after all.

The school is located on the south side of the city near Country Club Plaza. A couple of people from St. Louis said the school is near a "bad" neighborhood, but I didn't see it. Yes, if you live in Wildwood and you're not used to city neighborhoods, it may seem intimidating, but we found the area to be much like the Central West End — lots of museums, historic housing and lots of boutique retail and restaurants.

While we spent most of our time at the school, my daughter and I spent one night walking through the Country Club Plaza, a collection of 1920s Spanish-style buildings with shops and eateries. We stopped at a bookstore and while my daughter searched for books on French literature for one of her classes, I went straight to the "local interest" section. I found a chair and started paging through a history of Kansas City.

Much to my chagrin, I found out that the first settlement in the area was established by Francois Chouteau, a grandson of the founder of St.

Louis. Kansas City, it seems, could also be considered a proud French town. As far as music, I'd overlooked the fact that not only saxophonist Charlie Parker was a native, but also Count Basie, and, well, Eminem. Baseball? Yes, the Royals date only to 1968, but the city is also the birthplace of the Negro Leagues, which featured players such as Satchel Paige and James "Cool Papa" Bell. And Albert Pujols was drafted from a K.C. high school. Writers? I found out Ernest Hemingway cut his literary teeth at the Kansas City Star. And the city was named for the tribe of Kansa Indians well before the state of Kansas was established in 1861.

Before we left, I made a mental note of the places to see the next time I'm in Kansas City. Downtown, Crown Center, Union Station, the museums… and maybe even a barbecue place.

TWO GRADUATIONS, SAME YEAR

"Welcome to the first day of the rest of your lives!"

I was in a crowded bathroom in the gym building at the University of Missouri St. Louis when I heard a loud young voice proclaim this. The voice was familiar. Several people laughed at the slightly cynical tone.

The bathroom was filled with young men in caps and gowns, adjusting their ties, combing their hair, getting ready to join the 600 or so people about to graduate.

The voice was that of my oldest son, ready to join the group as a newly minted degree-holder.

A few weeks later, I was in our own bathroom at home. I grabbed a tie from my closet and tossed it to my eighth grade son. He was hurriedly dressing for his own graduation from Cathedral Basilica grade school. "Dad can you tie my tie?"

This was a familiar ritual with my sons. There was no time to show him *how* to tie it, so I stood behind him and wrapped the tie around his neck as if I was tying my own. Later, during the solemn ceremony at the Basilica (the "new Cathedral" on Lindell Boulevard) I noticed that his collar was open and the tie still hung loosely below his neck. So much for fatherly guidance.

This was the first time we had two kids graduate in the same season, and it gave me a chance to compare two entirely different rites of passage.

The UMSL ceremony was impressive, filled with distinguished professors and a long parade of young men and women eagerly shaking hands with the chancellor and clutching their new tickets to adulthood.

It was capped off by a short, poignant and at times humorous address by Martin Duggan. Duggan is a veteran of St. Louis journalism who referees the assortment of curmudgeons who debate the politics of the day on the local television show *Donnybrook*.

During the ceremony, I scanned the large group of graduates and watched my son, suddenly looking so grown up. I remembered in February when he gave me an invoice from school to pay for some of the graduation expenses. "Do you really want me to 'walk'?" he asked. "It's no big deal." Oh yes it is, I thought, and that was the quickest check I'd ever written for any of my kids' education. It made me think of the old Woody Allen line: 90% of life is showing up.

Graduating from grade school doesn't have quite the import of matriculating through college, but it's an important milestone. Unlike cultures of old, which had recognizable initiations for those leaving childhood — like, say, wild deer hunts — this is about all we have. We dress up gawky pre-adolescents in caps and gowns and then they become gawky adolescents.

My son and his classmates did a good job "walking the walk" for the ceremony at the Cathedral, dutifully listening to the principal and pastor impart their wisdom, filing in and out, smiling for the cameras. Although I could almost feel them squirming underneath their gowns; when will this be over? When can we get something to eat?

I really don't remember much about my own graduations. I do recall a speaker in high school saying that "these are the best years of your life" and I thought: if that's the case, what is there to look forward to? And the only thing I really remember from my college graduation at the old Arena was when my Dad, who was a professor at St. Louis University, walked over and shook my hand when I was walking down from the stage.

Graduations are like other big ceremonies in life: they're really for other people, not for the participants. Sorry — that sounds just like another platitude you might hear in the thousands of commencement speeches that take place every spring.

You know, like it's the first day of the rest of your life.

BRAGGING ON MY BILLIKEN PARENTS

Two people in my family recently participated in commencement festivities at St. Louis University.

But they weren't my kids; my oldest still has three years before he graduates from college (on the four-year plan, I hope).

Actually it was my parents; they graduated from St. Louis University 50 years ago and received the College of Arts and Sciences Alumni Merit Award. Allow me to brag on them for a bit.

The award was "to recognize our graduates who make outstanding contributions to their communities." My father received an undergraduate and law degree from SLU and later worked in the administration and taught in the business school. My mother received an undergraduate degree, and has volunteered for many years on the College of Arts and Sciences Alumni board. But I'm sure the award also was for putting their three sons through SLU, including myself (four years, barely).

Probably the best thing for my parents about SLU,though, was that they met there and got engaged in St. Francis Xavier (College) Church. Later this summer they will celebrate their 50th wedding anniversary.

The award gave me the chance to revisit the campus and the new Busch Student Center. I'll skip all the old stories about "when I went to SLU" (my wife calls it "geezer talk"), but suffice it to say that the university has become one of the city's success stories, with its modern campus and nationally recognized academics.

I also had the chance to speak again with Fr. William Faherty, S.J., after whom the award is named. Fr. Faherty will be 90 years old this year, and he remains one of the school's most distinguished retired professors. Fr. Faherty, who taught history for years at SLU, has written more than 30 books on topics ranging from St. Louis history to the U.S. space program. He still speaks with the wit, intelligence and incredible memory I remember from my student days, especially arcane bits of trivia about SLU

What exactly *is* a "Billiken"?

"HEY DAD, WANT TO PLAY A POWER CHORD?"

One late-February Thursday night about 10:30 p.m., I found myself standing shoulder-to-shoulder with my two oldest sons, aged 17 and 19, in the front row of a Yonder Mountain String Band Concert. The show was at the Blue Note in Columbia, Missouri, close to the campus of the University of Missouri. The music was great, but when I looked around, I was the token "old guy" surrounded by hundreds of college students.

When my dad was 44 (my age now) it was 1977 and I was 17. At the time, my dad was a banker who wore a suit and tie to work. I could never imagine him attending a concert with me at the time, say, the Eagles or Jackson Browne.

The image of a dad with his sons at a concert also summons the image of an aging old hippie trying to be buddies with his teenagers. That's not the case, either.

I'm still the dad. I still yell at them about driving, girls, drinking and homework — but music has become a common ground for us.

Last fall, when I got home from work one day, my wife asked me to talk to my son. "He's had a bad day." What she meant was: you need to deal with this.

I trudged up to his room on the third floor. He was sitting on the bed, his head down. He was having problems at school and he had just gotten a speeding ticket. He seemed overwhelmed.

"Hey," I said. "Want to go get something to eat?" That was one way to get a kid to talk — offer food, preferably of the fast food variety. My son looked at me. "Naw, that's OK. Want to play guitar?"

I guess some fathers toss a ball to their sons, or take them fishing. We pick up guitars.

This is a relatively recent phenomenon. About three years ago, I got a call out of the blue from someone I knew in high school. "Hey," he said, "want to get together and jam?"

I literally hadn't talked to this guy since my freshman year in college, when I told him and three other guys that I didn't have time to keep our "band" together, such as it was.

In the 20 years since, I played music now and then with a beat-up acoustic guitar I kept under my bed, but career, marriage and kids kept it limited.

But the phone call came at a good time. Our youngest child was out of diapers, I'd done all the home improvement I could stand on our 105-year-old house, and my wife was supportive. So I started playing with a group of guys a couple of times a month. Some play golf or poker with the "guys"; music became my middle-aged hobby.

As I started accumulating music "stuff," my oldest son took some guitar lessons. My next son started playing the banjo. Before long, we had created a music room in our rambling old house with a cheap P.A. system, a drum set and an old 15-inch Yamaha amp. I have another son who plays bass, and a daughter on keyboards.

In some ways it was the perfect combination of hobby and family togetherness; my wife only complained when we played too loud, too late.

At first I was surprised about the music my kids liked. I had spent years following the trail of Emmylou Harris and Gram Parsons and branching out from there, listening to a mix of alternative country, folk and bluegrass. The same kids who yelled at me to turn off that "twangy" music were now playing it with me.

My dad never played a musical instrument, but when I was a kid he put up with my tortured clarinet practicing for the school concert band, my late-night guitar playing and the occasional basement jam session.

More importantly, it was his love of music that got this whole thing started. My brothers and sisters and I spent hours in the basement listening to his records: Johnny Cash, Simon & Garfunkel and even Herb Alpert. Even though he was a sophisticated city kid from New York, now a banker, he would drive around with country music on the radio. "That's the music of the people," he'd tell us. And then there were those times he took me to the symphony or got me hooked on a Saturday night jazz show on the radio.

Thanks, Dad.

ORDER THE CAP AND GOWN. PLEASE.

Next weekend my second oldest son graduates from Truman State University in Kirksville.

At least that's the plan.

When he was home last month for spring break, I asked him if everything was ready for graduation. I said it in an offhanded way, like "What did you have for breakfast this morning?" What I really meant was: "I hope you've taken all the right courses, paid all of your library fines and gotten all of the right papers signed, because I've made hotel reservations, and we're coming up." Kirksville is a nice enough town, but I wouldn't necessarily choose to spend a weekend there in May for the scenery.

Having kids in college is a learning process for parents, too. I remember all of the preparation when he first went away to school… were courses selected, did we make the housing deposit, did he have enough pairs of socks?

After 18 years of raising a child under your roof — making sure they get up for school and go to the dentist and find a summer job — it's a big leap to drop them off at college and hope they'll figure it out.

Slowly, as he's progressed through school, he's taken on more and more responsibility, and we've had to step back.

And it has worked well. He lived in a dorm for two years and then for a year in a small house with three other students. For the past year, he's essentially managed his own affairs, moving into a house with seven other kids, paying most of his own way through work, scholarships and financial aid. He's also decided on a major and taken all the required courses to graduate in four years (which these days is a notable accomplishment).

The irony of course, is that while you want your kids to become independent — that's your job, right? — it's also hard to let go. As proud as we are of our son finishing and taking care of details on his own, we still expect a call every Sunday night. When he got a job in Kirksville last summer in his field, we were glad for him, but we missed him so much that we drove up *there* and spent a week in his "rustic" college house. And I always secretly hoped that his girlfriends were from St. Louis so we'd see him more.

Now that graduation looms, I have to admit I'm still concerned if he's ready. When I asked him about it at spring break, he mumbled something about having to order his cap and gown.

"What?" I said, trying not to sound too concerned. "I got a post card saying the deadline was three weeks ago."

"Oh, don't worry Dad, they said we could still do it next week."

Oh no. I had visions of my son not being able to "walk with his class" or strolling up to receive his diploma in a t-shirt and flip flops. I know it's symbolic, but I'd almost rather he admit that he still had "one more math requirement" to take than he didn't order his cap and gown. Why? Because I had made hotel reservations last fall, members of our family were making special trips, and we were going to Kirksville no matter what. If nothing else, we could take pictures in front of the student union with my son *in his cap and gown*.

I didn't hear from him that following week, and I stifled the urge to call him. I had even told him I'd pay for the cap and gown. I was getting anxious and becoming convinced that he'd forgotten.

Which was silly. He had taken more than 40 college courses and hundreds of tests, written dozens of papers, suffered through finals, made the honor roll, spoken at college conferences, fed and clothed himself and called home most Sunday nights. Surely he could order his cap and gown. Right?

Another week passed. Then one day my cell phone rang. It was my son.

"Dad, I'm at the checkout line for my cap and gown. Can I have your credit card number?"

Sure, son. That's easy.

Update: my son graduated from Truman, wearing his cap and gown. He also wore sandals, but that's OK, he walked the walk. After having a party at his college house (the "hippie hotel"), right before we left for home, my son said something about having to finish one last paper before he could move out. I started to say something, but stopped; at least I had my pictures of him in his cap and gown.

CHICKEN JOURNAL:

THE CHICKEN CIRCLE OF LIFE

Last year was not the best one for the small chicken flock in our backyard. The population was reduced by half, leaving Chicken Jane, a six-year-old from the original group (and one tough old hen) and Yellow, who is two years old and is actually more buff in color.

Though one is too old to lay eggs anymore, these two feathered friends spend their days picking at the ground, digging holes and avoiding the various predators who lurk around the yard.

It was one of these predators, an obese and probably "sick in the head" raccoon that nabbed our chicken Biff. Biff had her 15 minutes of fame by appearing in the pages of the *West End Word* for awhile last year in the Where's Biff? column. Truth be told, Biff wasn't exactly wild about being put in a laundry basket and driven around the city, where she was unceremoniously pulled out of the basket and forced to pose with my kids. She even ran/flew away on Union Boulevard once and we had scurry to catch up with her before she hopped into traffic.

Even though Biff was full grown, she was no match for the Rambo-raccoon that lumbered into our yard one night. A trail of her feathers marked her path across the yard to an opening in the fence and we never saw her again. The kids were very sad and I tried to explain the "circle of life." It was small consolation.

Meanwhile, a couple of cats were snatched away down the street and the people thought they saw a raccoon. The mystery was solved one night when my neighbor Damon said he saw a very large raccoon on his back porch one night, moving listlessly, acting strangely. Damon told me this one evening when I had some small kids with me; when I asked him what happened to the raccoon, he smiled, looked at my kids and said he "took care of it." Enough said. Circle of life.

We lost another chicken last year quite suddenly. When my wife went out to feed them one morning, Rita was in the small nesting box where they lay eggs. She realized that Rita wasn't moving. She was either sleeping or... So my wife waited a few hours, went back out and Rita still wasn't moving. This was evidently the "big sleep."

It turned out Rita caught a "chicken cold" or some disease that can be fatal. I know this because I googled "sick chickens" and there were stories about these mysterious, fast-acting poultry diseases. But some of my younger kids suspected another cause of death; on a very cold day a week before Rita died, one of my older sons decided to power wash the chicken coop with a hose, and a few chickens got "into the way" and were soaked.

But we'll never know. We dug a nice hole for Rita and said a chicken prayer or two.

But there were also stories of survival. Unfortunately, one of the chicken predators lives in our house. It's our dog Sadie, a beagle-terrier mix, a "hound dog" who is genetically programmed to yelp uncontrollably and run like mad after any kind of bird. Since we let our chickens run loose in our yard, there's no way we can let Sadie go in the backyard with them. Even if we plead to Sadie that the chickens are "part of out family."

But one day one of my kids left the back door open and Sadie bolted into the back yard. After years of chasing umpteen birds and squirrels just out of her grasp, I'm sure Sadie thought this was her lucky day. Like shooting fish in a barrel.

I didn't see this myself, but I was told Sadie took off after Yellow and some of my kids took off after Sadie. There were feathers flying and Sadie barking and kids running and just as Sadie bit down on Yellow's tail feathers, one of my kids grabbed Sadie. Yellow escaped with a newly trimmed backside and a small cut. Sadie ended up with a mouthful of feathers and a severe scolding. It's kind of hard to tell a hound dog not to do what a million years of evolution has bred into its bones.

We worried about Yellow for awhile, but she seemed fine, and the feathers grew back.

The last incident happened on a sub-freezing night. People often ask us what we do for the chickens when it's so cold. Most nights, the chickens actually like it, after all, they're wearing a down coat! But if it gets down near zero degrees, the chicken's combs on top of their heads might freeze, so we have rigged up a heat lamp for their coop.

One morning my son went out to open the coop and he smelled an odor like, well, cooked chicken. Apparently the chickens had slept too close to the lamp or had backed into it to get warm. Parts of their rear feathers appeared singed, but again, they hopped out of the coop like nothing happened. Let's put it this way: chickens aren't the sharpest tools in the barn, if you know what I mean.

We're thinking about going to Soulard Market to get more chicks soon. After all we need more eggs. And with spring approaching, it's time for rebirth and to add another cog in that circle of life.

INDEX

ABOUT THE AUTHOR

Jeff Fister is publisher of the *West End Word* newspaper. He lives in the Central West End neighborhood of St. Louis with his wife Laura, some varying number of his eight kids, two chickens and a dog named Sadie. In answer to the "St. Louis question," he went to Chaminade High School. He also graduated from St. Louis University and sometimes he sneaks away to play in his band Maxx Roby with some of his high school friends.